The
Honeymoon
Book

·THE·
HONEYMOON BOOK

Paula Scher

M. Evans and Company, Inc., New York, New York 10017

Acknowledgments

Some very special people helped me conceive and execute this book. I would like to thank Katy Hall McMullan for her original idea, my editor, Fred Graver, for his confidence in me and tireless efforts, Seth Shaw and Neil Flewellen for the mechanical work, Bob Felsenstein for the hand coloring on the cover, Marvin Frankel for the cover production, and Phil Haber and Haber Typographers Inc. for their marvelous typography. I would also like to thank the entire CBS Records Art/ Packaging Department for putting up with me while I was making this book, and a very private thank you to Robin Van Loben Sels.

MAKIN' WHOOPEE Lyrics by Gus Kahn/Music by Walter Donaldson—Copyright 1928 Donaldson, Douglas & Gumble, Inc. Copyright renewed and assigned to Gus Kahn Music Co. Used by permission of the copyright owner.

HONEYMOON HOTEL/© 1933 WARNER BROS. INC. Copyright Renewed
All Rights Reserved/Used by Permission

SHUFFLE OFF TO BUFFALO/© 1932 WARNER BROS. INC. Copyright Renewed
All Rights Reserved/Used by Permission

LET'S DO IT/© 1928 WARNER BROS. INC. Copyright Renewed
All Rights Reserved/Used by Permission

"The Real Life Honeymoon of Lucille Ball and Desi Arnaz. Adapted from p. 115-119 in A BOOK by Desi Arnaz. Copyright © 1976 by Desi Arnaz. By permission of William Morrow & Company

HOTEL ROOM © 1958 Cornell Woolrich. Excerpts reprinted by permission of the Chase Manhattan Bank N.A., executor of the estate of Cornell Woolrich.

"The Two Honeymoons of Jacqueline Kennedy Onassis, adapted from JACKIE O! by Kitty Kelly by permission of Lyle Stuart Inc.

"Complaints of Married People" by permission Harcourt Brace and Jovanovich, 1969.
Source: T. L. Engle and Louis Snellgrove, Psychology: It's Principles and Applications.

"Two Time Honeymoons" adapted from "Split Affinities—10 Couples Who Married Each Other Twice" from THE BOOK OF LISTS #2 by Irving Wallace, David Wallechinsky, Amy Wallace, and Sylvia Wallace Copyright © 1980 by Irving Wallace, David Wallechinsky, Amy Wallace, and Sylvia Wallace. By permission of William Morrow & Company

Library of Congress Cataloging in Publication Data

Scher, Paula
  The honeymoon book.

  1. Honeymoon.   2. Honeymoon—United States.
I. Title
GT2798.S33   392'.6   80-27900

ISBN 0-87131-339-1

M. Evans and Company, Inc.
216 East 49 Street
New York, New York 10017

Design by Paula Scher
Manufactured in the United States of America

9 8 7 6 5 4 3 2 1

For my Mother and Father

CONTENTS

CHAPTER ONE

THIRTY DAYS of DRINK

The Origin of Honeymoons and Assorted Other Tales

Another bride,
Another June,
Another sunny honeymoon,
Another season,
Another reason,
For making whoopee.

To the strains of *Lohengrin* they march down the aisle, their friends and family nodding in approval. She trembles at the altar. Her betrothed clasps her hand in his own. Their eyes meet and lock in an embrace.

Her mother is weeping. *His* mother is weeping. Their fathers noisily clear their throats. The groom searches for the golden wedding band, while his best man calmly taps him on the shoulder and hands him the ring. Nervously, the groom proceeds to clumsily push the ring on the third finger of the bride's left hand. The golden band halts at the bride's knuckle, to her momentary embarrassment. After what seems an eternity, the ring miraculously slides into place. Now she is his. Forever.

The bride and groom kiss, he with ardor and she ceremoniously, ever conscious of the presence of the wedding party and guests. They shyly turn to greet their family and friends and the wedding festivities begin.

As the evening's feast and celebration proceed, the bride and groom long for the moment when they can slip away from the bridal party and begin their honeymoon. Soon they bid farewell to their raucous friends and family— who shower them with rice and their good wishes. The groom's car has been decorated with streamers, tin cans, and shoes. A Just Married sign adorns the rear window. The bridegroom ushers his new wife into the car, climbs in on the other side, and merrily drives away. They are closely followed by noisy, drunken members of the wedding party who are yelling, whistling, and honking their car horns, and in general making an outrageous commotion. Onlookers smile at the uproar. Ah, newlyweds.

At the hotel, the groom nervously registers as Mr. and Mrs. for the first time, while the bride delights in her new name. The porter carries their bags to the bridal suite and waits for the bridegroom to clumsily lift his new wife and carry her over the threshold. The honeymoon has begun.

A Gallery of Brides.

What happens in the room that night is really none of our business, but we all have a pretty good idea of what is going on in there. Weddings make sex acceptable to us, and honeymoons are a celebration of sex.

♥   ♥   ♥

The term "honeymoon" is defined as a holiday spent together by a newly married couple, or any initial period of ardor and enthusiasm. In ancient marriages of capture (and still not such a bad idea) the groom kept his bride in hiding to prevent angry relatives from finding her, thus originating the concept of the honeymoon trip. But the word "honeymoon" is actually derived from the fact that those bawdy, newly married Teutonic couples ran off into the night and drank a fermented honey drink, mead or metheglin, for thirty days, or until the moon waned. The honeymoon could have just as easily been called the "mead month," or for those less euphemistically inclined, "thirty days of drink." It is fortunate for us to be left with the term "honeymoon," which is so lyrical and romantic (though there is still a lot to be said for "thirty days of drink," which sounds like a hell of a good time).

The wedding ritual originated as an exchange of property. That is not to say that the idea of love did not enter into the transaction. It was simply easier to love your wife or husband when you really didn't have that much choice in the matter. The bride was literally "given" to the groom by the father of the bride, or head of the bride's household. The parents of both bride and groom arranged the marriage. The bride's parents paid for the wedding and also provided a dowry and/or a trousseau. The word "trousseau" has its derivations in the French *trousse,* which means "bundle." Originally, a bride took a bundle of clothing and personal belongings with her to her new home. She was considered part of that bundle. The bundle of clothing was later expanded into a more generous dowry, which enhanced the value of the prospective bride in the eyes of her suitors.

Even a healthy dowry, though, was hardly a reasonable exchange for the lifetime financial burden of the bride. What evened out the marital deal was the possibility of the bride's fertility. If a bride could bear sons, the groom's family would gain field workers, merchants, warriors, or whatever kind of help the family needed for its own survival. If daughters were born, they would be

married off—with a little luck—and in the meantime they would help out in the household. So the marriage contract was seen as a positive bargain for both families.

Roman Bridegroom Leading His Bride To The Alter.

Something Old, Something New

All wedding customs have evolved as symbols of the sealing of the marriage bargain. They depict the many good things that marriage holds—among them, fertility, constancy, and happiness.

♥ The Ring ♥

The engagement ring, first known as the betrothal, or pledge, ring, was originally given as partial payment for the bride. It was a symbol of the groom's good intentions.

The earliest pledge rings were made of braided grass. Later ones were fashioned from leather, carved stone, and crude metals. The diamond, a noble stone, was first incorporated in engagement rings in medieval Italy because it was the most imperishable of all gems and thereby the ultimate symbol of enduring love. The circular shape of the ring also symbolized love-never-ending, a concept handed down to us by the early Egyptians (though the Egyptians themselves wore rings of braided rushes or hemp, which had to be replaced every year). Early Romans wore more durable iron rings, and more affluent medieval societies wisely preferred the purity of gold.

Betrothal rings and wedding bands are worn on the third finger of the left hand because the early Egyptians believed that the vein of that finger ran directly to the heart. Medieval bridegrooms placed the ring on three of the bride's fingers in turn, to symbolize the Trinity. They would recite, "In the name of the Father, the Son, and the Holy Ghost," and by the Amen the ring had slid neatly into position forever on the third finger of the left hand.

The English Prayer Book of 1549 wanted no confusion in ring position, and stated flatly that the third finger, left hand, was the proper and holy place for all wedding bands. The Greeks, in an act of defiance, completely ignored the English Prayer Book and the Greek women wore their ring on the left hand, switching it to the right after saying "I do."

♥ The Bride's Assets ♥

It should be mentioned that a great part of all this marital bargaining and deal making depended on qualifications of the bride other than her dowry: her health, her apparent (if untested) ability to bear children, and her chastity. Chastity was an important requirement, not only for religious reasons (everyone wanted a Virgin Mary), but also for the mere fact that nobody wanted to

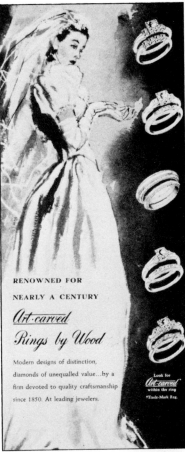

RENOWNED FOR NEARLY A CENTURY

Art-carved
Rings by Wood

Modern designs of distinction, diamonds of unequalled value...by a firm devoted to quality craftsmanship since 1850. At leading jewelers.

Look for *Art-carved* within the ring
*Trade-Mark Reg.

A German Bride and Groom ca. 1500.

A Chiness Bride and Groom Prepare to Retire for "Three Days of Seclusion" ca. 1850.

buy damaged goods. Brides went through a lot of hoopla to prove that they were chaste.

The bridal veil was considered a sign of youth and virginity. The veil originated in Greek and Roman civilizations. Ironically, the Greek and Roman women wore flame-colored veils, which would seem to denote passion, lust, and questionable morals if not out-and-out promiscuity. Early Christian women wore classic white veils, though for some strange reason purple veils ranked second as a popular favorite, suggesting passion mixed with possible violence. Anglo-Saxon brides hid their blushes behind their own flowing hair, while Jewish brides shaved their heads (so they would be beautiful only to the husband). It was often the case in Middle Eastern countries, and still is today, that the groom met the bride veiled, and never saw her until she was legally his. (That made for surprising honeymoons.)

In the United States bridal veils were introduced as a fashion by Nellie Custis, who started the rage when she chose to wear a long scarf at her wedding to President Washington's aide, Major Lawrence Lewis. Her idea stemmed

A Wedding Gown by Erte.

A French Wedding Procession ca. 1800.

Egyptian Wedding Dresses.

from the flattering comments her fiancé had made after getting a glimpse of her through a lace curtain at an open window. The rest of the young republic's brides followed suit. Nobody remembers whether or not Nellie was a virgin.

The color blue has always been a Judeo-Christian symbol of purity and virginity. Ancient Hebrew brides wore a blue ribbon on their fringed robes as proof of their chastity, and the Virgin Mary is most often depicted wearing the color blue.

Brides, insisting that they were a tremendous bargain, often tried to prove that they were chaste, fertile, and faithful—all at the same time. So they decked themselves out with symbolic flowers, hiding them under their gowns, wearing them in their hair, or carrying them in bouquets. Orange blossoms were a big favorite among the Saracens because the orange tree blooms and bears fruit at the same time, thus exquisitely capturing the flavor of youth, purity, and fertility, in one bud. Lilies were considered the flowers of purity, and roses were the "love blossoms." The Greeks added a little touch of ivy, which represented indissoluble love, because you could never be too careful.

● Showers ●

There is a legend from Holland about a young maiden who was very poor and had fallen in love with a well-to-do miller's son. The maiden's father had forbidden the marriage because he could not afford to pay the dowry that the miller demanded. The maiden would be forced to marry into a poor family like her own.

The spirit of love, of course, conquered all. The miller's son's friends saved the day by "showering" the maiden with gifts so that she could set up a traditional household despite her lack of dowry, and the bridal shower was born. (She received thirty-two blenders and a toaster oven.)

A lot of shoes. A lot of rice.
The groom is nervous.
He answers twice.
It's really killing,
that he's so willing,
For making whoopee.

● Wedding Symbols ●

Because weddings were a public exchange of property, the celebration of the exchange was also public. All society knew that the authority over the bride had changed hands. Among the early Hebrews, sandals were often given as evidence of good faith in any property exchange. The shoe was a European symbol of domestic authority, so it follows that it has become an important symbol in weddings.

In Anglo-Saxon marriages, the father of the bride demonstrated the transfer of authority by taking the shoe from his daughter's foot and handing it to his new son-in-law. Upon receiving the shoe, the groom became the bride's

An Indian Car Decorated for a Wedding.

new owner and master. To show off his new authority, the groom would hold up the shoe and lightly tap the head of the bride three times. (Surely, this was the origin of love taps.) We have modified the custom somewhat over the past ten centuries. Now we tie shoes to the back of the honeymoon car.

The word "bridal" comes from "bride-ale." In medieval times the family of the bride was allowed to make ale and sell it on the wedding day, thus combining business with pleasure. It was a nice way for the father of the bride to raise money for the dowry and wedding expenses, as well as keep his guests appropriately rowdy while they celebrated the "sealing of the bargain."

The wedding cake has been a must in wedding celebrations since the early Romans, who broke a thin loaf over the bride's head at the end of the ceremony. The wheat from which the loaf was made was a symbol of fertility, and the crumbs that came tumbling down were eagerly gobbled up by the wedding guests who believed them to be good luck.

In England during the Middle Ages, it became traditional for a bride and groom to kiss over a pile of small wedding cakes, to insure that they would procure an abundance of healthy offspring. At that time, some enterprising baker got the idea to mass all the cakes together and cover them with frosting. *Voilà!* The modern tiered wedding cake.

The wedding guests enhanced the future fertility of the bride by pelting the departing couple with rice. The custom stems from the Orient, where the throwing of rice is equivalent to saying, "May you always have a full pantry." It is an interesting analogy.

FROM ITS LOOSENED FOLDS THERE POURED A STREAM OF RICE.

Honeymoon Folklore.

A Czechoslovakian Wedding Procession.

If an ex-lover, with hatred in his heart, kisses the bride on her wedding day, her honeymoon will be an unhappy one. —Old Proverb

The honeymoon has been considered "the first sweet month of Matrimony," as evidenced by all that drinking. Since the purpose of honeymooning was to ensure proper marriage consummation, virginal brides, ever superstitious, looked for every possible good luck omen.

It was considered good luck for a bride to take something borrowed with her on her honeymoon, as a link to her past life. The Roman bride, demonstrating a true virgin's reluctance to leave her father's household, had to be literally carried (kicking and screaming all the way) over the threshold of her new home or wedding-night retreat.

Some brides believed that there were evil spirits lurking over the threshold of the honeymoon abode, so the bride not only saw to it that she was lifted over the threshold, but often insisted that the marriage be consummated away from the future home. Hence, wedding trips were planned, and all the young couples ran off to drink.

Once inside the honeymoon chamber there were other superstitions to observe. If the husband climbed into bed first, he would outlive the wife, but the first one to fall asleep would be the first one to die. (Fortunately, no one sleeps on honeymoons, anyway.)

The following was a prescription for good luck and longevity: "Take a pound of Limburger cheese and spread it between two towels to make a poltice. Place it under the pillow of the newlyweds on their first night together, and good fortune and prosperity will be theirs."

If the Limburger-cheese method proved excessive, the bride and groom could sleep with their heads pointing north, and good luck in the future was all but assured.

On the morning after the wedding (assuming the evening had been a success), it was customary for the bride to have the privilege of asking for the "morning's gift." The bride could ask for any sum of money or piece of property that she desired, and if it was within the husband's means, he was honor-bound to give it to her. If the husband could not afford her request, it was his responsibility to make another offer. The "morning's gift" had to be honored at some time in the near future, and would become the basis for the wife's economic independence. (The better the wedding night, the bigger the gift.)

A Smashing Honeymoon <u>or</u> How to Break In a Marriage

Since everyone assumed that the consummation of marriage was also the deflowering of a chaste virgin (unless, of course, the bride was a widow or divorcée), there were all sorts of rituals designed to ensure that the blossom was plucked without a hitch. As a symbolic gesture before the honeymoon was in full swing, all kinds of objects got broken, smashed or shattered.

In Europe, they broke eggs, earthenware vessels, and objects of glass. The English threw wine goblets over their shoulders, while the Jews stomped on them, smashing them to bits.

An old Irish custom had a bridesmaid hurry to the honeymoon chamber before the arrival of the bride and groom. She poured a glass of beer (Guinness, no doubt) and handed it to the groom after he had lifted the bride over the threshold. The bridegroom proceeded to chug-a-lug the beer, tossing the empty glass behind him. If the glass broke, the evening would be a success.

Germans were known to break all sorts of pottery outside the bridal abode. They believed the more shards, the better the honeymoon. Sometimes they got totally carried away and started breaking the windows of the honeymoon house. A great deal of shattered glass meant sexual success, and wealth as well.

The Serbs of Serbia were the biggest voyeurs in honeymoon history. At midnight, the head of the groom's family would usher the blushing bride into the groom's room. The groom was already unclothed and in bed. The father of the groom would then bolt the door of the bridal chamber and guzzle a glass of wine. The empty glass would be shattered against the honeymoon door. The wedding party would cheer the breakage and the imminent loss of the bride's virginity.

While the Serb bride and groom remained in the privacy of their quarters, the guests would continue to make an uproar, breaking glasses, pots, and anything else they could get their hands on. They would throw the objects at a burlap sack that contained an egg and was laid against the wedding chamber door. While the guests were busy smashing everything in sight, one of them would inadvertently break the egg in the sack. When the egg was broken, the marriage was determined officially consummated.

The Chivaree was a popular custom in the United States in the seventeen and eighteen hundreds. It consisted of a band of friends and wedding guests who would follow the newlywed couple to their honeymoon haven. They would stand outside the bedroom and serenade them, unless, of course, the guests were drunk, which was usually the case. Then they would be rowdy

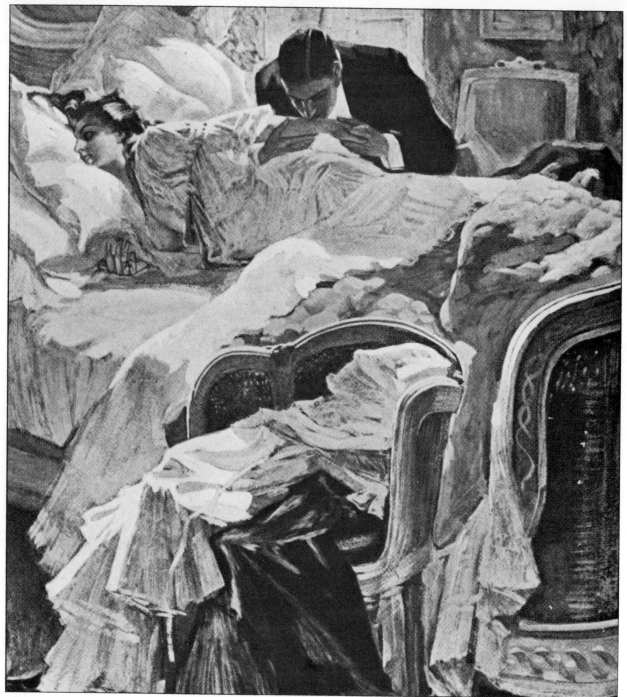

"The Morning After"

and irreverent, carrying on and making general fools of themselves. Unlike the Serbs, if they broke anything, it was usually just a drunken accident.

Among various northern African societies, a rod, staff, or tree was smashed—in a little reverse symbolism. (European countries nearly always smashed cups, glasses, and vessels.) The wedding parties of North Morocco outdid everybody in terms of the most dangerous honeymoon ritual. When a Moroccan bride was led to her honeymoon haven, she rode on the back of a mule, holding up a cane with a red flag fastened to the end of it. The male members of the wedding procession fired shotguns at the cane, hoping to blow it to bits. If the cane was shattered, the bride's hymen would (symbolically) be broken, and all would be well.

The color red, so frequently used in wedding celebrations, is the ultimate symbol of the deflowered virgin. The Chinese Cantonese suspended three long strips of red paper from the canopy of the nuptial bed to extend good wishes to the consummating couple. The Greeks and Romans provided inspiration and incentive to their honeymooners by dressing the bed in red satin sheets. The Finns left nice white sheets, so the couple could be proud of their handiwork, but they laid down a red blanket as a reminder of things to come in the night. Just about everyone toasted the honeymoon couple with red wine—or pink champagne for partial virgins.

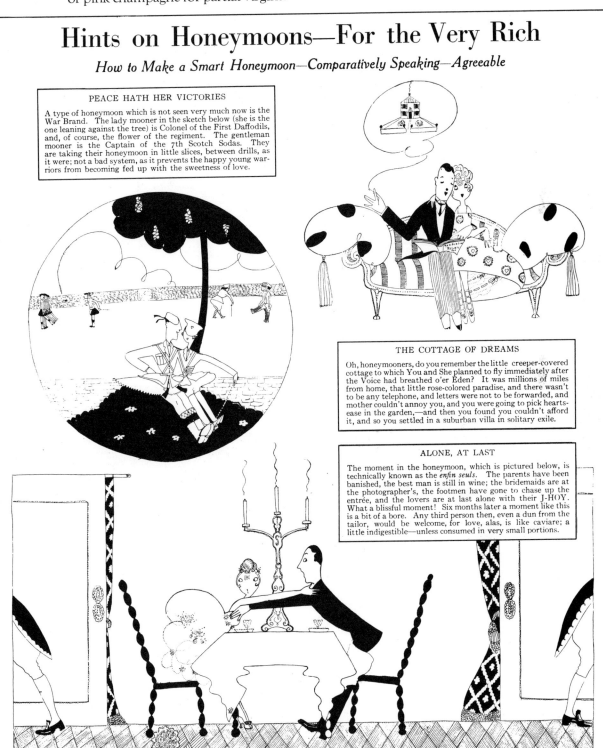

Hints on Honeymoons—For the Very Rich

How to Make a Smart Honeymoon—Comparatively Speaking—Agreeable

PEACE HATH HER VICTORIES

A type of honeymoon which is not seen very much now is the War Brand. The lady mooner in the sketch below (she is the one leaning against the tree) is Colonel of the First Daffodils, and, of course, the flower of the regiment. The gentleman mooner is the Captain of the 7th Scotch Sodas. They are taking their honeymoon in little slices, between drills, as it were; not a bad system, as it prevents the happy young warriors from becoming fed up with the sweetness of love.

THE COTTAGE OF DREAMS

Oh, honeymooners, do you remember the little creeper-covered cottage to which You and She planned to fly immediately after the Voice had breathed o'er Eden? It was millions of miles from home, that little rose-colored paradise, and there wasn't to be any telephone, and letters were not to be forwarded, and mother couldn't annoy you, and you were going to pick heartsease in the garden,—and then you found you couldn't afford it, and so you settled in a suburban villa in solitary exile.

ALONE, AT LAST

The moment in the honeymoon, which is pictured below, is technically known as the *enfin seuls*. The parents have been banished, the best man is still in wine; the bridesmaids are at the photographer's, the footmen have gone to chase up the entrée, and the lovers are at last alone with their J-HOY. What a blissful moment! Six months later a moment like this is a bit of a bore. Any third person then, even a dun from the tailor, would be welcome, for love, alas, is like caviare; a little indigestible—unless consumed in very small portions.

Anne Boleyn

Catherine of Aragon

Jane Seymour

Anne of Cleves

Catherine Parr

Catherine Howard

CHAPTER TWO

The SIX HONEYMOONS of HENRY VIII

Had King Henry VIII of England remained married to his first wife, Catherine of Aragon, it is likely that the Holy Roman Empire would still be ruling the Western World. But Henry dumped or beheaded most of his six wives because none of them produced what he most wanted for his kingdom—a healthy male heir to the throne.

In the process of his wife dumping, the ruthless "Great Harry" succeeded in decapitating much of the clergy and intelligentsia of England, who had opposed his marital willfulness. He also managed to break relations with the pope, leaving himself in a politically vulnerable position at home and abroad. Finally, he gaily set about establishing the Church of England, placing himself at its helm. All for the want of a son!

Never before, and never again, had a nation's political and religious climate been so much affected by the bedroom life of its ruling monarch. But the fact that forty years of marriage, with six different wives, could produce only one sickly legitimate male heir for Henry and the English crown (Henry's third wife bore him sickly Prince Edward, who wheezed and coughed his way to an early grave) does seem a remarkable twist of fate.

It is common knowledge that Henry was fully capable of siring healthy male offspring because he had done so with Bessie Blount, and numerous other wenches as well. He could produce bastards, but no legitimate heir, and he thought he had been cursed by the devil.

A modern analysis of Henry's troubles would remind us that Henry had always bedded with his legitimate wives in his various castles and courts, or at the manors of powerful political friends and allies—hardly private or relaxing environments for lovemaking, with the whole castle aware of what they were doing and when. It would have been as private and relaxing to tryst in the public square! Whereas when King Henry bedded with his wenches, he went off to fields and farms, far away from the burdens of the monarchy. Those adulterous evenings were respites of pure pleasure.

So when we consider Henry's enormous burden of achieving successful fertile intercourse with his legal wives, before all of England and Western civilization, it is easy to understand why he was incapable of producing more legitimate children. It must surely have been enough performance pressure to wilt the sword of the mightiest and most virile warrior.

Any modern psychiatrist would have advised King Henry simply to "relax, take a trip, get away from your problems. Go someplace quiet and romantic, and don't take any phone calls."

What Henry needed, in other words, was a good honeymoon. A little "thirty days of drink" in the Bahamas would have probably resulted in the birth of a healthy male heir before the year was out. The course of English history would have been altered, and countless heads would have remained attached to their necks.

How cruel it is that we cannot rewrite history in retrospect. But there is a fascination in pondering "What if—?" The following is a sampling of plausible honeymoons befitting both King Henry and the tastes and idiosyncrasies of his wives.

♥　　♥　　♥

The Trial of Queen Catherine of Aragon

CATHERINE OF ARAGON

Catherine of Aragon, Princess of Spain, was the widow of King Henry's older brother. Henry married her shortly after his brother's death, having obtained a dispensation from the pope in order to establish that this was not an incestuous liaison. The pope granted the dispensation because of his alliance with Spain, and because he had accepted Catherine's sworn statement tht her previous marriage had been unconsummated and, therefore, illegal.

Queen Catherine and Henry were married for twenty-four years. Catherine suffered a series of miscarriages and stillbirths (all male) during the marriage, finally giving birth to her only surviving child, Mary. Several years after Mary's birth, Henry became obsessed with his lack of a male heir. Though he respected Catherine and, in fact, had great affection for her, he began directing his romantic attentions elsewhere—most notably, to Lady Anne Boleyn. At this point, Catherine was too old to attempt to bear any more children.

As Henry's infatuation with Anne Boleyn grew, he blamed Catherine for his lack of heirs, believing that their marriage had been cursed because he had entered into an incestuous relationship with his brother's widow. Despite Catherine's protests of chastity and innocence, he demanded of the pope that he be granted a divorce.

The pope refused. A previous pope had granted dispensation for Henry to marry Catherine. The new pope, who happened to be related to Catherine, was not about to reverse the old ruling.

Willful Henry decided to ignore the pope. He broke relations with the papacy and established the Church of England. He demanded that all his subjects agree to take an oath stating that his marriage to Catherine was invalid and that her daughter was a bastard.

Thomas More, who was then Lord Chancellor of England, refused to support the king and subsequently lost his head. So did many other devout Catholics, who were punished for being heretics.

Catherine, of course, refused to acknowledge the divorce, nor would she allow her only daughter to be declared a bastard.

Catherine died several years after Henry's divorce and remarriage, alone, living in house arrest. Her daughter, Mary, would spend the rest of her childhood and adolescence in the country, or at court, in disgrace. She would finally assert her right to the throne and seek her revenge.

Honeymoone for Queen Catherine Of Aragon and King Henry

on the Splendid Isle of Wight

My Lord, pray goeth,
To the misty bounding main,
And here ye shall knoweth,
Faire lady Catherine of Spaine,
And by the grandeur of near dune,
Spendeth blessed honeymoon,
Midst true gardens of delighte,
On the splendide Isle of Wight.

Whilst seaspray cooleth thy regal face,
And faire maiden whom thou wed,
O'er the sands shalt ye embrace,
On hilltop castle shall ye bed.
Maketh thy honeymoone a loving paragon,
For thy royal Highness, and thy Queene from Aragon.
Still falleth the night
On the splendide Isle of Wight.

Pray, cometh, Lord Highness, to the sea,
Forgetting thy burdens, thy royal cares.
And by the sunlight, merry be,
And by the moonlight, maketh heirs.

• THY ROYALE HONEYMOONE •
(From thine own humble servants on the Isle of Wight)

By the merest pittance of one thousand crowns per day, your Royale Majesty doth delighte in all pleasures e'er created for mortal man. Had the angels knowne faire days and nights to be so fanciful, they wouldst surely hath flung themselves from the heavens. Eight days of magic and bemusement awaiteth thee, on this splendide Isle of Wight.

♥ FEASTING ♥

A sampling of the finest cooking and cuisine, by the most revered chefs of thy majesty's realme, awaiteth thee—nay once, nor twice, but any mealtime as ye desireth. Thy feasts be an eight course meal, prepared as is your Grace's pleasure. Thou canst enjoy our pheasant from Calais, roasted in ambrosia, quail from our faire forests, trimmed with truffles, or chooseth South Hampton duckling, roasted with cherries, fresh fishe caughte dailye (our specialtye be pinkest salmone) or selecteth roasted wilde boar with apples. Thou canst always request our grandest soufflés or cakes or pies, tarts or scones, soups or stews, or the freshest fruites of the orchard and field. Each repast shalt end with our complimentary royale goblet, filled to the brim with holy meade, sweeter than the wine of angels. We shalt toast thy royale health, prosperity and blissful honeymoone.

♥ JOUSTING ♥

Be day or dark nighte, we shalt transporteth the bravest knights of thy kingdom and worlde to perform feats of bravery for thy Royale Highness and the faire Queene Catherine. These bold knights wilst begin to joust or wrestle or decapitate one anothere as his Majesty sees fit and doth commandeth. For thine own entertainment and pleasure your Liege may challengeth such said knights to feats of bravery and courage that he desireth. Fear not, O Royale Highness, for on this splendide Isle of Wight, our Great Harry always the victor shall be.

♥ MUSIC AND SINGING ♥

Thy Grace shalt be enchanted by our finest and most musical minstrels of voice, lute, lyre and harpsichord, as he doth commandeth. Thy minstrels performeth at thy royale beck and calle, at any hour, morne or nighte. Ye shalt be serenaded at thine own sweet pleasure, be it whilst feasting, sunbathing or bedding.

THE
SANDS AND SEA

Thy royale cabana awaites thy Liege, for the pleasures of swimming and sunbasking. The seas be madeth safe for thy great Highness by the royale guard who doth watcheth o'er thy Grace. Ye shalt fear not the warme waters, for thou shalt be protected from all harme. Valets of bathe and chamber awaiteth thy return from thine own regal plunge, to dowseth thee with freshest spring water, and washeth away the darke sea's salty brine. Thou shalt be patted dry by our richest and most velvety cloths. Then shalt ye be tenderly caressed and massaged with royale softening ointments of rosemary and cocoa. A faire skinned King shouldst caress his Queene.

♥ FISHING ♥

Royale fishing vessels awaite thy Majesty's command. They shalt be equipped with our most able, brave and capable fishermen to escort and aide your Grace. Thy royale catch shalt be cleansed and cooked for thy dining pleasure, at thy Majesty's request. Our faire seas be abrim with shining mackerel, healthy red snapper, fairest pink salmone and gaye oysters. Thy sturdy fishing vessels are crafted only with our finest woods, silver and gold.

♥ HUNTING ♥

Thy forests be laden with wilde deer, elk, boar, quail and bear. Thou mayest hunt with thy choice of weapon, knive, saber, rifle or that of a great archer. The blackest and whitest of stallions be madeth ready for thee in the royale stables. As his Majesty is the strongest and bravest horseman and huntsman, then maketh his pleasure knowne. Excellent hunting companions bid thee welcome, and thee may stalketh prey to thine own heart's content. His Highness's kill shalt be cleaned and prepared for thine own feasting, shouldst ye be desirous of this thing.

♥ BEDDING ♥

Our majestic hilltop castle was builte as a fortress for King Henry II and be it equipped for a Liege as grand as our fine Harry. The floors be crafted with grandest marble and stone. Our ceilings be carved and of magnificence. Our stairways be curved and sure. Thou canst bed in two adjoining chambers. Faire Queene Catherine ne'er be far from her royale lover, yea, shouldst his majesty desire this, there be a private chamber near the kitchen shouldst the activity of wenching occur.

Thy royale mattresses hath been made up of the softest down of duck and geese, and likewise the pillows. Silken sheets maketh up the beds, whilst ye shalt lie beneath coverlets of fox and ermine. All thy royale necessities of bath and chamber be decorously attended by our royale valets. Make thy bath in marble tubs of the shape of hearts and engraved in gold with "H" and "C" entwined as a lover's knot. For thine own secret pleasures thy royale honeymoon bed bears in its canopy the clearest looking glass, inlaid on its ceiling.

♥ PRAYING ♥

A holy Cathedral of golden magnificence be only footsteps away from thy royale dining hall. The bishop of Kent and his holiness, the Cardinal of Rome, doth journey long and far to be at attendance and of assistance for thy royale prayers. These holinesses be available to serve as companions and loyal instructors to Queene Catherine. They are a comfort to her piety, as thy Majesty doth amuse himself with hunting, fishing or wenching. Mass and Communion are celebrated each morning, or by thy Grace's commandment.

ANNE BOLEYN

Henry was captivated by Anne Boleyn, who was cultivated, charming, and shrewd. Anne was not a great beauty, but she was of noble birth and had exquisite bearing. She had watched amorous Henry woo and seduce half the noble women of his court, and she had no intention of adding her name to the list of his conquests. Marriage was her price for sexual favors, and she held back her charms until her goal was assured.

Anne was pregnant when she finally married Henry, and Henry asked his subjects to love Anne and recognize her as their queen. But the English subjects resented Anne Boleyn for destroying Henry's previous marriage, and their church. They labeled her "the Great Whore."

Henry was well aware of Anne's unpopularity, but he assumed all would be well when Anne bore him a healthy male child, which she did, but the infant died only hours after birth.

At the time of Anne's second pregnancy, Henry had already tired of her, and had begun to return to his old ways. Anne bore Henry a healthy daughter, Elizabeth, but Henry was not pleased. He began to look for ways to rid himself of his second wife. She was still widely hated, and Henry now considered her to be a witch.

Henry enlisted the aid of Thomas Cromwell, whom he had recently appointed Lord Chancellor, to help him find a way of dumping Anne Boleyn. Cromwell had been helpful previously in the divorce of Catherine of Aragon.

Anne was now in her third pregnancy and well aware that her marrige would be short-lived. The third birth was, understandably, premature, and resulted in another stillborn male. Anne's days were numbered.

Meanwhile, Henry had become smitten with another noblewoman, Jane Seymour. He urged Cromwell to get him out of the Boleyn marriage posthaste. Cromwell trumped up a few phony adultery charges against Anne. She was brought to trial, and though the court could actually prove no wrongdoing, they convicted her of treason anyway Boleyn was sent to the Tower and lost her head shortly thereafter.

The daughter, Elizabeth, was declared a bastard and exiled from the court. The skill at escaping danger and death that young Elizabeth necessarily developed during her childhood would serve her well when she became Queen of England.

A Honeymoone for Queene Anne Boleyn and King Henry in Sherwood Forest

Come, gaily hide in the merry woode,
And forgetteth mortal man.
Spendeth thy dayelight as Robin Hood,
And spendeth thy nighte in Anne.
Thou hast patience, for she didst give in,
(A stubborn wench, faire Anne Boleyn).
Yea, the future bears thy sons for sure.
Why else shouldst thou marry the Great Whore?

Yea, in the wood, thou canst feast and sing.
Nay, sad thoughts of Catherine, left in the lurch.
Pray, merry amusement the morrow shall bring,
And a gaye farewell to the tyrant pope's church.
So, Sherwood Forest shalt host thy pleasure,
Of lust, and love, and peace, and leisure,
And the seeds of future kings doth begin.
Why else wouldst thou marry this Anne Boleyn?

Yea, liveth like outlaws in the merry woode,
And by thy love, serve thy kingdom good.
And pray for sons as you nighttime bed.
For if faire Anne shouldst fail you, then off with her head.

• THY ROYALE HONEYMOONE •
(From thy obedient knaves of Sherwood Forest)

Come, and hide away in the wood, for a secret fortnight of love and peace. Yea, at the most inconsequential fifteen hundred crowns per day, we doth judiciously make thy respite safe and quiet. Be at rest, as in days of old when brave Robin and his Merry Men ruled the wood. The forest kingdom be thine, and all the pleasures therein.

♥ FEASTING ♥

Thou doth dine on thine own rich kill in the great rock cave by the trickling stream. Nay, the cave is nary a hideout of a mere outlaw, nor a home for barbarians, but a fine mead hall, as resplendent for King Henry as 'twas fit for young Richard-the-Lion-Hearted. Thou shalt be served and soothed by maids certainly more beauteous than faire Marion, and all attired in robes and clothe of the grand Thirteenth Century. Thou tasteth fine old wines, and feasteth on freshest game. (Wilde pig and duck be the specialty of the forest, both served with succulent wilde berries.)

♥ ENTERTAINMENT ♥

For thy Majesty's amusement and pleasure, we stageth the "great robbery" (on the hour or the half hour). His Majesty, and a band of thieves and cutthroats (selected by thy Grace from thine own gallant robbers at our local prison), lay in waiting on a dark forest hilltop. A troupe of wealthy merchants (all finely attired and bejeweled) maketh their way down the grassy forest path to meet their fates of ultimate ambush. They be startled by thy Majesty (who cloaked as Robin be). Thy band and thy Majesty dueleth with the inept merchants, and through great courage and skill doth easily defeat them. Ye then demandeth their wallets and jewels, which they mercifully hand over to thee in exchange for their lives. If one foolish merchant doth refuse his disguised Majesty's command, then your Lordship shalt slay him for treason. All the great loot shalt then be donated to our own poor as faire Robin wouldst surely have done. Yea, the finest bauble may be given as a token to faire Anne Boleyn, who wouldst appreciate thy great generosity. After the ambush, thou proceedeth to the campfire by the great cave to drink and sing and make merry.

• HIKING •

On faire and lazy an afternoon do walketh through the thick forest, on lightly beaten pathway, with the faire Anne on your arm. Ye shalt not knowe the danger that lives there. At any moment, thou may be surprised by the evil Sheriff of Nottingham, who hath lain in waiting for thee and thy queene. Fear not, O master swordsman, for thou canst certainly outwit him. Shouldst the cruel Sheriff capture faire Anne, thou only needeth pursue him and fight for thine own dear lady. Thou shalt be hero and saviour unto Anne, for which she wilst surely reward you, come the twilighte.

• BEDDING •

Steppeth up to thine own hidden tree-house for thy bed and thy bath. Thee shalt be waited on in a princely fashion by thine own band of thieves. They shalt attend to their own true leader's every need and desire, whilst sweet Anne shalt awaite thee in a secret room upon the piney staircase. (The wedding chambers doth adjoin.) Sleepeth on bedboard fashioned from walnut and cedar. Breatheth the fresh forest air. The pillows be freshly stuffed with feathers from geese shot down by thy majesty's own hand. Thy coverlets be soft bear and wolf skins. Thy wooded floor holds rugs of deer and elk hide. As thee beds, ye shalt be serenaded by thine own band of thieves who sing jolly songs of days of yore.

• PRAYING •

Thou shalt be led in prayer by thine own defrocked Friar Tuck. This monk doth accepteth thine own Majesty as true head of his sacred church. Thou shalt kneel on satin pillows by the Virgin Mary, in thine own holy cave where thou readeth the scriptures by torchlight.

JANE SEYMOUR

Jane Seymour was the most frail of Henry's wives, and it is ironic that she would bear Henry his only surviving male child. Having been raised in a monastery, Jane was devoutly Catholic and was greatly distraught at the treatment the monks and nuns had received when Henry formed the Church of England.

Though Jane was neither ambitious nor willful, her quiet, loyal ways had a profound effect on Henry. During his marriage to her, he ceased his harassment of the Catholic clergy, and England enjoyed a rare period of religious peace and unity. An added bonus to England was the successful birth of a legitimate male heir, Prince Edward. Henry's joy in that birth was followed immediately by tragedy when fair Jane died of complications of childbirth.

Henry genuinely grieved Jane's death. (He later requested that he be buried next to her.) Prince Edward's health was guarded most carefully, and very few members of the court were allowed into the royal nursery for fear of contaminating the infant prince.

Though England finally had its heir to the throne, Henry was still justifiably dissatisfied with the safety of his succession. Prince Edward was a sickly child. He ultimately survived Henry and assumed the throne, but only for a short time. He precariously wheezed his way through sixteen mucus-ridden years, when he too died.

A Honeymoone for Queene Jane Seymour and King Henry

in a Deserted Monastery

Whenst thy Grace doth marry his faire, sweet Jane,
Pray cometh to thine own Abbey,
And redeemeth thy heart and soul again.
Yea, blessed thy holy honeymoone be.
For God surely smileth upon his grace,
And pure sweet Jane's most noble face.
He shalt forgiveth all annulments didst come before.
Our own true Queene be faire Jane Seymour.

Yea, joineth our monastery and live as a Friar,
Do knoweth God's presence as ye woo and bed.
Harken, O Lordship, come sing in our choir;
For sons surely cometh from where thee wed.
And Jesus doth smile upon thy great realm,
With thy royal Majesty and faire Jane at our helm.
Take no saddened looks towards dark days of yore,
For our own true Queene be faire Jane Seymour.

Yea, here in thine own holy abbey stay.
By daylight pray for sons, by moonlight pray for play.
And thine own gentle Jane shall be faithful unto thee.
The Lord's blessing be thine for a nominal fee.

♥ ♥ ♥

THY ROYALE HONEYMOONE

(From thine own devoted monks of God and King)

Thy Majesty shalt passeth a faire week in monkly piety and holiness with thine own beloved Jane, and seeketh all the heavenly joys of sanctuary herein. For a humble donation of seventeen hundred crowns per diem, thy Royale Highness may redeemeth his own soul, and knoweth thy Lady Jane as thou doth begin holy matrimony. Thy loyal monks shalt attend to thy every wish and desire.

♥ FEASTING ♥

Thy Grace doth dine as a simple Friar on our own fresh produce from the Abbey farms: great white eggs, finest of fowl, freshest milk and the holiest wine. All meals shalt commence with prayer for thy Majesty's health, and the speedy production of his heirs. Our monks shalt serve thee, and serenade thee with Christ's own hymns. Thy royale repast doth conclude with the nightly reading of thy Highness's own Holy Bible, and a goblet of sacramental wine.

♥ PRAYING ♥

Thine own Majesty and thy Queene Jane doth partake in the most rigorous morning prayers led by a holy Cardinal of thine own choosing. Our own abbe be simple yet holy. Thine own prayers be modest yet heard and answered. A secret mass be prepared for thy Grace before thy morning prayers.

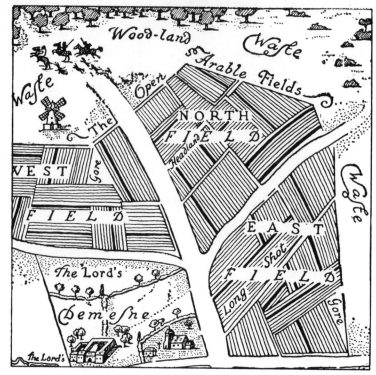

Thy Majesty shalt enjoy these simple pleasures of holy farming life as ye and faire Jane doth throw feed to our own chickens, and milketh our cows. For his Majesty's pleasure there be the great afternoon hayride through our own rolling countryside. (Our holy barns be available for a regal roll in the hay.) His Majesty canst pick reddest apples from our holy orchards and tasteth sweetest berries of our holy bush. The pleasures of field and pasture be thine.

♦ BEDDING ♦

Thy Royale Highness shalt bed as thy monks hath done, on sturdy wooden frames, with fine homemade mattresses and pillows. Thy blankets be woolen and of great softness, as they were woven here in our monastery from the coats of our own sheep. Our monks will attend to thy private needs of bath and chamber as well as thy nightly prayers.

♦ SLEEPING ♦

Thine own monks shall pray for your happiness whilst thou sleep, and surely God doth visit thy holy bed chamber.

♦ READING ♦

Thy Grace shalt be allowed the peace and solitude of all friars, as he doth escape to our holy library, for the pleasures of reading and thought. Our library containeth all important works of mortal man and Holiest Christ. During this period of solitude, faire Queene Jane shalt amuse herself as a nun, and retire to our sewing room for her needlepoint and quilting.

♦ THEOLOGY ♦

We will daily present revered and important members of his Majesty's clergy, to debate the finer points of theology with his Royale Highness. His Majesty shall feel free to contradict all foolish viewpoints, and he shalt winneth all debates. Our own true Majesty be the highest authority on God and Man.

ANNE OF CLEVES

After Jane's death, Henry lost some of his appetite for womanizing. Now in his midforties, he was losing his robust appearance and his health. He had also developed gout, which would plague him for the rest of his life.

Lord Chancellor Cromwell was determined that Henry should remarry, and was convinced that England needed an alliance with a strong Protestant nation in order to ward off continual threats from Spain, France, and the Holy Roman Empire.

Out of a bevy of German princesses, Cromwell handpicked Anne of Cleves to be King Henry's fourth wife. The great portraitist Hans Holbein was commissioned by Cromwell and sent to Germany to capture Anne's beauty on canvas. A very flattering portrait of Anne of Cleves was presented to King Henry.

Henry liked what he saw. He agreed immediately to a new betrothal and began passionately corresponding with his new bride-to-be. Henry's messengers told Anne romantic tales of the king's physical perfection, his courtliness, and his grandeur. She was soon excited and anxious to meet her new husband.

Anne was brought to England where she was given a grand apartment at court, and she impatiently awaited her first meeting with King Henry. In a festive mood of romance, Henry decided to surprise Anne by turning up at her apartment disguised as a messenger from the king. When Henry revealed himself to Anne, she was horrified that her husband-to-be was a stout, stale-breathed, gout-ridden old man. Her horror was apparent, and an insulted Henry left her apartment in disgust.

"I like her not!" he raged at Cromwell. But Henry was persuaded by all his advisers that for England's political security he must proceed with the wedding.

Anne of Cleves was in quite a predicament. She did not want to marry this man, and she certainly did not want to go to bed with him. She knew the history of Henry's previous wives and feared for her life. She was resolved to get out of this marriage amicably, and as soon as possible.

Anne was kinder to Henry on their next meeting. She was understanding of his political difficulties (she was exceedingly bright and well educated), and she showed Henry the empathy of a true and great friend. She reasoned that to show the Holy Roman Empire the firm resolve of England and Germany as allies, they should go through with the wedding, but there was no reason to consummate their marriage since they were not attracted to each other.

Henry succumbed to her logic and agreed to her plan. Soon, he also became enamored of her. After their marriage, he chased her around the castle while she gently reminded him of their bargain. Her diplomatic skills showed true genius. Their marriage was indeed never consummated and ended a year later in an amicable annulment.

Anne of Cleves had done the impossible. She had kept her chastity, her head, and her apartment at the king's court. Cromwell was not so lucky. He lost his head for his abortive attempt at matchmaking.

A Honeymoone for Queene Anne of Cleves and King Henry in Historic Antwerp

Yea, now thou doth marry our faire German Queene,
Though thy heart beats not, and thy mind meanders.
So cometh to see what thou never hast seen,
And spend thy honeymoone here in Flanders.
For Antwerp, oure fine German towne, serves thee well.
So come tasteth our wine, and ringeth our bell.
Rejoice in oure hamlet, forgetteth thy peeves,
Thou couldst do worse than marry the faire Anne of Cleves.

Yea, here in great Antwerp, thou shalt know and bed her,
As part of thine own fine political plot.
'Tis Cromwell's fault that you wenteth and wed her.
For he shouldst hath knowne ye wouldst like her not.
But in a week, in Antwerp, with thine own new Queene,
'Tis possible to see what Holbein hath seen,
For surely didst he paint her portrait faire.
There be more than thou knowest to this fine Flanders mare.

So droppeth thy protests, and give Anne thy heart,
And here in great Antwerp, we shalt do oure part.
For what thou doth giveth, in kind thou receives,
Thou couldst do worse than marry the faire Anne of Cleves.

• THY ROYALE HONEYMOONE •
(From thine own new friends of historic Antwerp)

For the smallest token of two thousand crowns per day, oure faire city be thine, and all the services and pleasures therein. The grande towne of Antwerp doth awaite thee in all the grace and splendour befitting thy great Sire and thy travelling party.

♥ FEASTING ♥

Each repast shalt be an orgy of merriment and delight. We do set our great long tables for his Majesty and thy Aides with our finest pewter, silver and gold. The tables be laden with oure greatest sausages and bolognas, fowl, breads, and cheeses: all from oure faire city. Thou shalt be attended by maids merry and rotund, who doth cajole thy Majesty and wilst surely amenably bed with thine own wedding party, shouldst they be desirous of this thing. Tasteth our great beers, which we breweth in the neighbouring countryside. Dineth on our freshest fish, caught daily in the great locale rivers. All feasts shall be accompanied by singing, dancing, debauchery and delighte.

♥ SIGHTSEEING ♥

Antwerp beeth a fine olde hamlet. Thy Majesty canst traverse oure fine olde canals, whilst oure gaye townsmen and women shall line the banks to wave and cheer thee. Visit our beautiful windmills and oure faire tulip fields. (There be no finer place to pursue and woo the faire Anne.)

• ENTERTAINMENT •

We bringeth the greatest and wittiest fable tellers from all the land to amuse his Royale Highness with rhyme and reason. Thy Majesty doth be delighted with such great stories of witchery, sorcery, bravery and immorality. Oure most imaginative fable makers shalt create a legend of his Majesty's own sacred marriage to oure fine Queene Anne, and shalt predict thine own bountiful and fertile future.

• WARRING •

For the pleasure of his Grace's purse we shalt organize our bravest knights, and preparest them to invade and conquer a piece of the Holy Roman Empire that his Majesty doth desireth. Oure knights canst invade any Duchy in France or Spain as your Grace shalt request. The loot from oure great victories shalt be returned to your Highness's court as part dowry payment for the faire Queene Anne. Shouldst his Majesty wisheth to join us in oure merry invasion, then cometh gladly.

• BEDDING •

His Grace shalt retire to oure finest olde German Inn, which doth grandly accommodate thy Highness, the Queene and thy royale wedding party. Thy chambers be great and beautiful, filled with freshest flowers and fruits of the field and trees. Thy bedding chamber doth also contain thine own private wine closet. Drinketh and maketh merry before bedding, and leave the night to love. Oure faire Queene be modern and broadminded and shalt allow thee a fleshy maid or two to warm up thy royale bed.

• MEDICINE •

There beeth oure most proficient medical attendants to swathe and bathe thy Majesty's ulcerous leg. We useth only the fresh ointments that cometh from herbs and flowers. If the horror of bleeding needst occur, his Majesty shall be anesthetized by oure strongest beverages of alcohol. Ye shall feel no pain.

• PRAYING •

We be a Protestant land, yea, we supporteth his Majesty's own Holy Church and Bible, and we shalt prepare a secret mass for his great Highness each morning in the Catholic tradition that his Grace doth prefer.

CATHERINE HOWARD

Catherine Howard was the niece of the powerful Duke of Norfolk, and cousin to Queen Anne Boleyn. After Henry's annulment from Anne of Cleves, Norfolk realized that he had an opportunity to gain favor and power from King Henry, by seeing to it that the now-bachelor king marry into his family.

Young Catherine was eighteen, lovely and vivacious. Aging Henry was easily smitten with her. They were betrothed almost immediately after their first meeting. Unfortunately, Catherine neglected to tell either her uncle or the king that she was not chaste, and had once had a young lover. Catherine felt that this was unimportant, that Henry would never find out, and that she would be a loyal and faithful wife to her king.

Young Catherine was also delighted at the idea of being queen. She loved the jewels she had received from Henry as a betrothal present, the majesty of the king's robes, and the grandeur of the palace court.

But Catherine was in for a shock on her wedding night. When his Majesty disrobed, she was horrified at his aged, ravaged body. She dutifully tried to lure him into lovemaking, but the king merely wanted to look upon her.

For Henry, Catherine was a fountain of youth. His aides claimed that Henry's spirits improved the moment Catherine entered the room he was in. He obviously adored her, and showered her with more jewels, and land as well.

Catherine was not pleased. Henry's impotence both disappointed and threatened her. She felt that if she did not provide an heir for him he would soon become bored with her and she would be discarded. She foolishly planned to give him an heir through other means and began taking on lovers.

Catherine proved as indiscreet as she was unwise. Soon the court was abuzz with the young queen's infidelities. When the Duke of Norfolk heard of his niece's transgressions he feared for his own life as well as the lives of the rest of his family. He realized that he had no choice but to inform the king of Catherine's unfaithfulness.

Henry was genuinely heartbroken. He felt like an old man. He banished Norfolk from court but did not claim his title or his head. Catherine fully confessed her treason and was sent to the Tower. She was executed, and Henry was left alone with his bitterness and his gout.

A Honeymoone for Queene Katherine Howard and King Henry at the Fountain of Youth in Florida

So, Lord, taketh now thy sweete young Kate,
And bed her manly, never coward,
For great sons shalt cometh from this faire mate,
Wisely thy Highness didst weddeth a Howard!
And in sunny Florida learneth this truth,
That age be not the key to youth.
So love through the daylight, and lust till the dawn,
Thy foul leg be healed, thine arthritis be gone!

Now, late in life thou doth find thy peace,
But thine own sweete love be worth the waite,
Since thou wisely didst weddeth Norfolk's niece,
Ye shalt findeth thy youth in this lovely Kate.
So spendeth faire days by oure Florida waters.
And the nights shalt bring sons, nay, no more daughters!
So woo in thy tent, and roll in the clover,
Thy foul breath be sweetened, thy gastridous be over!

Yea, thy health be robust, and thy praises be sung!
Thy love be the truest, and thy heart beats young!
So live as our liege, but love as a lad,
And findeth the body his Grace always hath had!

THY ROYALE HONEYMOONE ❧
(From thy friendly Spaniards of Florida)

Pray, Lordship, cometh to this beauteous fountain of youth, as the Great Ponce de Leon hath done. Here thou canst romp and play and regain the once powerful physique that we knowest thou to have. For the most insignificant sum of twenty-five hundred crowns per day (plus the expenses of thy Majesty's ocean crossing) thy Royale Highness canst love, woo and heal thyself in a true garden of Eden, at the world's most famous health spa.

❧ YOUTH'S FOUNTAIN ❧

Cometh and soak in our cool healing spring waters and tasteth their magic sweetness. Youth's fountain shall reviveth and purify thy royale body. Thy Majesty shalt be spry and active and ready to woo his faire young Kate! Though thy Majesty may entereth youth's fountain as an aging warrior, he shalt emerge as an Adonis with his sword mighty, and his heart full of life. The magic fountain is secluded and romantic. Ye shall bathe in privacy, and woo in the reeds!

❧ GRAPE NIBBLING ❧

His Majesty doth dine on all the natural aphrodisiacs of heaven, earth and sea. Suck luscious oysters, lick succulent clams and feel thy spirits rise. Taste of our natural fresh fruits and their potent nectars. Drinke the fine wine of Spanish grapes or nibble upon the raw grapes themselves, as they be peeled for sucking by thy loyal and friendly natives. All such ambrosia is only a prelude to love.

✦ CAVORTING ✦

Thy Highness and Queene Catherine shall cavort within our tropical forests under the care and protection of thy loyal Indian slaves. Fear not fierce crocodiles nor slippery alligators, as all natives are superb harpoonists who wilst gladly see to thy safety. Thy Majesties shouldst stroll 'neath a lace canopy of netting to protecteth thy royal bodies from fierce and deadly insect bites.

♥ EROTICA ♥

Thy Highnesses shalt be inspired by tribal dances of naked warriors who perform their rituals for your secret lusts. Harken to the native drumme beat and its great pulsating sensuality. Thy Majesties shouldst enjoy adorning themselves with the beads, feathers and war-paint of our native tribes, to perform thy own personal ritual dances. Live like Indians at the Fountain of Youth.

♥ BEDDING ♥

Thy graces shalt bed within a great tent, constructed and woven from our finest and softest silk. Yea, the beds shall be great and heavy Spanish beds of feathered down. Oure Indian slaves doth quietly and judiciously attend to thy sleeptime and bath needs, and do fanneth thy sleeping Majesties, if thou doth care to sleep, and swat away all pesty insects. Before bedding thou shalt be served a complimentary glass of mango nectar. 'Tis said that this was the aphrodisiac of the gods. Oure slaves shalt also anointeth thy bodies with sweet coconut oil to prevent the dryness of thy skin from our Florida sun's merciless rays.

♥ PRAYING ♥

Catholic mass will be held daily in oure locale missionaries, and his Majesty and Queene Catherine shalt be granted their private mass. The missionaries are honored to attend to thy Godly needs upon his Highness's request.

♥

Our Royale King of Spain sends his fondest regards and honeymoone wishes for a healthy and fertile marriage.

CATHERINE PARR

Catherine Parr had been widowed twice when she married Henry. She was a comely, well-educated woman who married her king in his golden years to serve as his friend and companion.

Catherine Parr was under no pressure to bear children or even be Henry's bed-mate. Henry had finally accepted his own impotence and decrepit condition. He anticipated no more heirs, and hoped to live out the rest of his life in peace.

In the beginning, Mrs. Parr's definite opinions about religion and politics rankled Henry. She was often labeled a heretic by some members of Henry's court, and many were disturbed about her influence and power over the dying king and considered her dangerous. But Catherine quickly learned diplomacy and soon began to control her tongue. She became greatly involved with the well-being of Henry's children and was largely responsible for their education.

After Henry's death, Catherine Parr remained in court as an undeclared "queen mother." She was actually more powerful after Henry's death than during their marriage.

A Honeymoone for Queene Catherine Parr and King Henry in Brighton

Your Grace hath journeyed long and far,
The winds blew cold, the storms didst rage,
So find thy peace with Catherine Parr,
And calmly liveth an olde, olde age.
Yea here in Brighton stop to rest,
And leave us serve each royale request,
And as you wish, it will be so,
For Brighton Beach is where olde people go.

Faire Catherine Parr will love you well,
And careth for the royal heirs ye sired.
Now taketh thy rest! Thy life was hell!
'Tis only just that thou shouldst be tired.
So here in Brighton cometh sit a while,
And be loved and served in regal style.
Yea, laze, and lie, and wasteth the day,
For Brighton Beach be where olde people stay.

'Tis time to twiddle, and twaddle, and tarry,
And find peace and comfort from where thou didst marry.
Catherine be gentle, 'tis wise thou didst wed her,
With the greatest of effort, ye mightst even bed her!

♦ THY ROYALE HONEYMOONE ♦

(From thine own humble, non-complaining, apolitical servants of Brighton)

For the worthy fee of three thousand crowns per day, thy Majesty and thy Queene doth benefit from all the luxuries, pleasures and comforts from thy regal hotel accommodations at Brighton. Cometh to our majestic shores and leave us soothe and care for thee.

♥ FEASTING ♥

We doth prepare a host of thy Highness's favorite dishes, with thine own best health interests at oure hearts. The food be delicious, but prepared in a manner less rich than that to which thy Majesty hath been accustomed. We do this thing in deference to thy Grace's ulcerous leg, and rising cholesterol level. We serveth the leanest of beef, the simplest of fowl, freshest of fish and finest veal, but we serveth no butter or other dangerous fats. Thy Grace doth quench his thirst on our purest mineral waters, for thy digestion and constitution. Thy meals be excellent, but short, and unabundant. All repasts shalt be served by comely, yet hardly desirable maids, who concern themselves solely with thy Liege's health and well-being.

♦ WALKING ♦

After each repast, there willst be the post-feast stroll, wherein thy Majesty shalt be aided by nurses, in a slow walk about the room. If the day be faire, then thy Highness may stroll outside to a bench in the courtyard. These walks be necessary to aid in his Majesty's great digestion.

♥ NAPPING ♥

When thy Grace finish thy royal walk, thy nurses wilst lead thy Highness to thine own bed chamber for thy royal nap. Thy Highness shouldst nap one houre after each feast for to build the great constitution and prevent the exhaustion. Thy nurses doth permit thee to hold hands with Queene Catherine before falling asleep. If his Highness doth command it, then Queene Catherine wilst commence to read something uninspiring and inoffensive to his Majesty's intellect, before thou doth retire to thy royale nap.

• SITTING •

After thy royale nap, thy Grace shalt be led to a great soft chair by the ocean. Thy Highness shouldst sit under a royale sun umbrella to prevent sun spots from marring thy faire skin. Thy Liege may watch Queene Catherine bathe in the ocean, and mayst take a short walk to greet her, at the water's edge. Thou shouldst then return to the great chair and resumeth thine activity of sitting, to prevent thy fatigue.

• LAUGHING •

Thy Majesty shalt be amused for one hour, by the wittiest jesters and fools of the realm. Thy Grace mayst partake in laughter and joke telling shouldst he promise not to becometh too excited.

• BEDDING •

Thy Grace doth bed in the finest hotel chamber, and Queene Catherine doth bed in an adjoining room. The chamber be affixed with all of thy Majesty's ointments and medications on hand, and to be administered by thy royale doctors and nurses, who be always on call. Thy Majesty's chamber be sound proof, though there be a lovely view of the ocean. One night of the honeymoone, shouldst his Majesty be hardy enough, ye mayst bed with Queene Catherine, if she be desirous of this.

• PRAYING •

Archbishop Cranmer shalt be available at all times to administer Prayer, Mass, and Confession, as thy Majesty so requests. All Prayer shalt be administered in his Majesty's bed chamber.

THE AFTERMATH OF KING HENRY VIII

King Henry ultimately left England three heirs to the throne, though two were women. Sickly Prince Edward, the son of Jane Seymour, became a boy king at age ten and managed to survive a six-year reign, even though he wheezed and coughed his way through it all. He even made plans to marry his cousin, Lady Jane Grey. He planned a romantic marriage, and an illustrious honeymoon, but he unfortunately sneezed himself into an early grave before the wedding took place.

After a power struggle with Lady Jane Grey, Princess Mary, daughter of Catherine of Aragon, made her way to the throne. Mary married King Philip II of Spain, who was also her cousin. She angered all England with the match. The realm was not interested in another Spanish alliance, and they had had it with the Catholicism of the Holy Roman Empire. There was also no love lost between Mary and Philip, as Philip basically perceived Mary to be a tyrannical fool and wanted to rule England himself. Always the diplomat, however, Philip accurately assessed that the English people had no use for him, so he spent most of his marriage in Spain. Mary was decidedly anxious to avenge both her mother and the Catholic Church, so she spent her reign beheading Protestants and old enemies of her mother. She was aptly dubbed "Bloody Mary."

Bloody Mary was hardly a popular queen, and that kept Philip even further away. They were certainly, in no respects, a honeymooning couple, nor did they ever travel together, or take a honeymoon trip. Mary's pregnancies were all false ones, and soon the barren queen became sickly and died. She left the world an angry, embittered old woman.

Fortunately, Mary had appointed her half-sister, the Princess Elizabeth, as heir to the throne. Elizabeth was Anne Boleyn's daughter, and what she had seen of marriage had taught her to avoid it at all costs. She proclaimed herself married to England alone, and even wore a ring to prove it. Though she dallied with lords and dukes and foreign princes, her flirtations were empty, and her country remained her own true love. She died the pure, chaste, virgin queen.

When Elizabeth died, so did the Tudor reign of her father and her grandfather. Elizabeth had produced no heirs at all.

The fact of the matter remains that if Henry VIII had only bothered to take a honeymoon, the Tudor dynasty would be alive today.

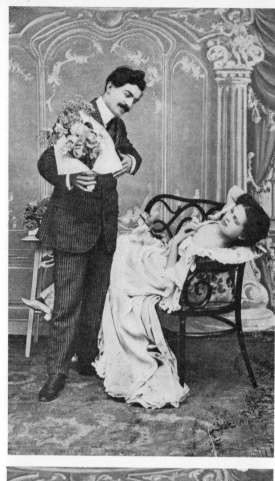
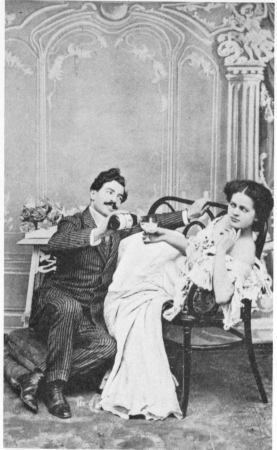

CHAPTER THREE

The VICTORIAN HONEYMOON
• or •
HOW TO HONEYMOON WITHOUT SEX

> There is great happiness and great blessedness in devoting oneself to another.... Still, men are very selfish and the woman's devotion is always one of submission, which makes our poor sex so very unenviable. —Queen Victoria on Marriage

Queen Victoria set the style and etiquette standards of her time, and as we can tell from the above, it was a very, very long time. We are, in fact, still bearing the brunt of her moral codes today. She told women that sex would be no fun at all. Sexual intercourse became an unpleasant necessity in which well-bred women participated only as a marital obligation. Of course, unmarried women did not participate in sexual activities at all, for fear of a ruined reputation and becoming a social outcast.

Victorian brides decided that the wedding night was a necessary evil, so they held their noses, closed their eyes, and bravely submitted to their husbands in the honorable Victorian manner. They hoped that, with a little luck, their brutish beastly mates would contain themselves and be gentle. They paid their price for holy matrimony, and they were probably a real bundle of joy on a honeymoon!

Yet, if sex was really so distasteful, the question remains why more women didn't simply avoid marriage altogether and become nuns or spinsters. Fortunately for them, the brutish men still controlled business, the media, and the tourist industry. They sugarcoated honeymoons and turned them into glamorous wedding tours, involving the purchase of expensive new finery for the blushing bride. Depending on the wealth of the newlyweds the "wedding tour" could be as lavish as a six-month cruise and a visit to the entire continent of Europe, or, at the very least, a stay at the finest new hotel in the nearest metropolitan capital. (Those too poor to afford even the latter were probably not of the well-bred classes, and simply had no compensation for having to succumb to disgusting animal lust.)

Hotel managers began accommodating newlyweds by creating bridal suites for the comfort of the "honeytourers." They also equipped themselves with a staff who could understand and deal with the little eccentricities of the newlyweds, such as the screams and cries of the ever resisting brides.

If a young bride had been fortunate enough to buy new shoes, hats, dresses, and parasols to accompany her on her honeymoon, the wedding night might pass as quickly as a bad dream, and all could be forgotten in the morning.

Victorianism concentrated on the aspects of romance and beauty in "love everlasting" as an antidote to the more disgusting terrors of the sexual experience. The following excerpts of romantic wisdom are from a book entitled *Light on Dark Corners*, which was first published in 1894 and was the most sexually enlightened book of its time.

♦ LOVE *and* COMMON SENSE ♦

Do you love her because she goes to the altar with her head full of book learning, her hands of no earthly use, save for piano, because she has no conception of the duties and responsibilities of a wife, because she hates housework, hates its everlasting routine and recurring duties, because she hates children and will adopt every means to evade motherhood? Will you love her selfish, shirking, calculating nature after twenty years of close companionship?

Do you love him because he is a man, and therefore, no matter how weak mentally, morally or physically he may be, he has vested in him the power to save you from the ignominy of an old maid's existence? Because you would rather be Mrs. Nobody, than make the effort to be Mrs. Somebody?

♦ OR: ♦

Do you love her because she is thoroughly a womanly woman, for her tender sympathetic nature, for the sweet sincerity of her disposition, for her charitable thought, in brief because she is the embodiment of all womanly virtues?

♦ AND: ♦

Do you love him because he is a manly man, because the living and operating principle of his life is a tender reverence for all women, because he has never soiled his soul with an unholy act, because physically he stands head and shoulders over the masses?

There have always been, and always will be, unhappy marriages, until men learn what husbandhood means, how to care for that tenderly nurtured, delicately constituted being that he takes into his care and keeping. That if her wonderful adjusted organism is overtaxed and overburdened, her happiness, which is largely dependent on her health, is destroyed.

Until men and women recognize that self-control in a man, and modesty in a woman, will bring mutual happiness that years of wedded life will only strengthen, until they recognize that love is the purest and holiest of all things known to humanity, marriage will continue to bring unhappiness and discontent, instead of that comfort and restful peace which all loyal souls have a right to expect and enjoy.

Be sensible and marry a sensible, honest and industrious companion, and happiness through life will be your reward.

Which Will It Be?

♦

◄ Hotel Room ►
from the book of that title
CORNELL WOOLRICH
The Night of June 20th, 1896

They followed the bellboy in and looked around.

"Oh, it's nice, isn't it?" she said.

"Yes, it is, isn't it?" he agreed.

The bellboy bustled around, trying to make unnecessary actions look like highly necessary ones. Then he retired to the door and came to the crux of the matter. "Will there be anything else, sir, for now?"

"No, thank you." Young Compton put something in his hand a little self-consciously.

The boy eyed it with widening eyes. "Thank you. Thank you very *much,* sir." He backed out, closed the door, and they were alone.

The slightest of pauses followed.

Then she asked, "Did he bring everything up?"

"Yes," he said. Then he contradicted himself by amending, "Wait, I'll count," and told off each separate piece with outpointed finger. "One, two, three—and that little one. Yes, he brought everything up."

Another sliver of pause came between them; under other circumstances it would have been scarcely noticeable as such, but now they were acutely aware of every momentary silence that occurred between them.

"Don't you want to take off your hat?" he suggested with an odd mixture of intimacy and abashed formality.

"Yes, I guess I may as well," she assented.

She crossed to the dressing-table and seated herself at the glass. He remained where he was, watching.

"Gee, I always *did* think you had such pretty hair!" he blurted out suddenly with boyish enthusiasm. "The very first time I met you, I noticed that about you."

She turned her head and smiled at him, equally girlish to his boyishness for an unguarded moment. "I remember, I'd just washed it that day. And

● WHAT WOMEN LOVE in MEN ●

Woman naturally loves courage, force and firmness in men. The ideal man in a woman's eye must be heroic and brave. Woman naturally despises a coward, and has little or no respect for a bashful man.

LARGE MEN. Women naturally love men of strength, size and fine physique, a tall, large strong man rather than a short, small weak man. A woman always pities a weakly man but rarely ever has any love for him.

SMALL AND WEAKLY MEN. All men would be of good size in frame and flesh were it not for the infirmities visited upon them by the indiscretions of parents and ancestors of generations before.

SOFT MEN. All women despise soft and silly men more than all other defects in their character. Woman can never love a man whose conversation is flat and insipid. Every man seeking a woman's appreciation or love should always endeavor to show his intelligence and manifest an interest in the various topics of the day.

SEXUAL VIGOR. Women love vigor in men. This is human nature. Weakly and delicate fathers have weak and puny children, though the mother may be strong and robust. A weak mother often bears strong children if the father is physically vigorous. Hence, women love passion in men, because it endows their offspring with greater strength.

Young man, if you desire to win the love and admiration of young ladies, first be intelligent, remember what you read, so you can talk about it. Second, be generous and do not show a stingy or penurious disposition. Third, be sensible, original, and have opinions of your own, and do not agree with everything someone may say, or agree with everything a woman may say.

The Two Paths

What Will the Girl Become?

AT 13 BAD LITERATURE	AT 13 STUDY AND OBEDIENCE

AT 20 FLIRTING AND COQUETTERY	AT 20 VIRTUE AND DEVOTION

AT 26 FAST LIFE AND DISSIPATION	AT 26 A LOVING MOTHER
AT 40 AN OUTCAST	AT 60 AN HONORED GRANDMOTHER

⌐ Hotel Room ⌐

Mamma had helped me put it up afterward. I told her that night how lucky it was we had."

She turned back to the glass and looked at it intently in there. "It must be terrible to grow old and have it turn gray. I can't picture that; the same hair, like it is now, should turn gray and still be on *me*."

"But everyone's does when they get old enough."

"Yes, other people's; but to have it happen to *you!*" She peered at herself more closely. "I can't imagine it ever happening to *me*. But when it does, it won't be me any more. It'll be somebody else." She touched her fingers to the sides of her face. "An old lady looking out of my eyes," she said wonderingly. "A stranger inside of me. She won't know me, and I won't know her."

"Then I'll be a stranger too," he said thoughtfully. "Two strangers, in a marriage that was begun by two somebody-elses."

For a moment they were both frightened by this thing their nervously keyed prattle had conjured up. Then they both laughed, and the imminent fright went away.

He went over to her and touched his lips to the piled hair on the top of her head. She acknowledged the caress by placing her hand atop his, where it rested lightly on her shoulder.

"Are you tired?" he murmured close to her ear.

"Yes. Not—too much, though. Just from all the excitement."

Then he suggested, "Why don't you sit down? No sense standing."

She selected an armchair, deposited herself into it with a little bounce of possessiveness, due in part no doubt to the newness of the springs. She said again, as she had about the closet, "Oh, I'd love to have a chair like this when we have our own home."

He slung himself down beside her on one arm of the chair, and tucked his arm around her to her further shoulder, and feeling it there, she allowed her head to pillow back against it.

They were quiet for some moments, utterly, blissfully content. No need to talk, nor even to caress. Their being together like this, close like this, was in itself one big caress. He allowed his head to incline toward hers at last, that was the only thing, and remain there, cheek pressed to the top of her head.

She said softly, "I can't believe it even yet, can you?"

He understood the unexpressed thought. "No," he said. "Me either."

"That there was a time, only a little while ago, when there wasn't any you yet, just me. By myself, alone."

"And now there's you and me, both."

"It must be terrible to be alone."

"Like we were a couple months ago."

"I can't remember it any more, can you? But it must be terrible. To go through each day without any—you."

"But now we don't have to any more," he said. "From now on, each day has you in it."

He took out a watch. She'd seen it before. It had been given to him on his graduation from high school. He'd told her so. It was gold-plated. He'd told her so. It had a fob of two little pennants of black moiré ribbon. They hung from an inch-wide bar. That was gold-plated too. It was the only watch they had with them, but one was enough. They had no separate needs of time; there was no time apart from one another. There was only time together.

He opened the lid with a spunky little click. She loved to look at the lid. It was bright as a mirror. It had on it: "To John, from Mother and Dad."

He said, "I guess we better think about—" And then he stopped, because he hadn't been ready in time with the right last word. The sentence really called for the terminal phrase "—going to bed," but he didn't want to use that. She didn't want him to either.

He only stopped a moment; you could hardly notice it. Then he didn't go back over the first part again. He only said "—retiring."

"I guess we better," she assented.

He got off the arm of the chair.

Then he said, "I guess I better go downstairs a minute—first." Somebody must have told him this was the considerate thing to do. Maybe his

♥ WHAT MEN LOVE in WOMEN ♥

FEMALE BEAUTY. Men love beautiful women, for woman's beauty is the highest type of all beauty. A handsome woman needs no diamonds, no silks, nor satins; her face outshines diamonds and her form is beautiful in calico.

A GOOD FEMALE BODY. No weakly, poor-bodied woman can draw a man's love like a strong, well-developed body. A round, plump figure with an overflow of animal life is the woman most commonly sought, for nature in man craves for the strong qualities in woman, as the health and life of her offspring depend upon the physical qualities of wife and mother.

BROAD HIPS. A woman with a large pelvis has a superior and significant appearance, while a narrow pelvis always indicates weak sexuality.

SMALL FEET. Small feet and small ankles are very attractive because they are in harmony with a perfect female form, and men admire perfection. Small feet and ankles indicate modesty and reserve, while large feet and ankles indicate coarseness, physical power, predominance.

BEAUTIFUL ARMS. As the arm is always in proportion with the other portions of the body, consequently a well-shaped arm, small hands and small wrists, with full muscular development, is a charm and beauty not inferior to the face itself, and those who have well-shaped arms may be proud of them.

PIETY AND RELIGION IN WOMEN. Men who love home and the companionship of their wives, love truth, honor and honesty. It is the higher moral development that naturally leads them to admire women of moral and religious natures. It is therefore not strange that immoral men love moral and church-going wives. Man naturally admires the qualities which tend to the correct government of the home. Men want good and pure children, and it is natural to select women who ensure domestic contentment and happiness. A bad man, of course, does not deserve a good wife, yet he will do his utmost to get one.

FALSE APPEARANCE. Men love reserve and discretion in women much more than they admire some of the more modern womanly (?) characteristics. Falsehood, cigarette smoking, gambling and masculinity are poor foundations on which to form family ties.

The Two Paths

What Will the Boy Become?

AT 15 CIGARETTES AND SELF ABUSE	AT 15 STUDY AND CLEANLINESS
AT 25 IMPURITY AND DISSIPATION	AT 25 PURITY AND ECONOMY
 AT 36 VICE AND DEGENERACY	 AT 36 AN HONORABLE SUCCESS
AT 48 MORAL-PHYSICAL WRECK	 AT 60 VENERABLE OLD AGE

◅ Hotel Room ▻

father, maybe one of his friends.

"All right," she said tractably.

She had stood up, too, now.

He came close and he kissed her.

His face didn't have the handsome regularity of a Greek statue. But a Greek statue couldn't smile, couldn't show light in its eyes.

He went nearly as far as the door, but not quite.

Then he touched his pockets exploratively. His wallet, with his—their—money in it.

"I don't need this," he said. "I'll leave it up here."

He went over and he put it on the dresser-top. Not too far from where the necktie was, tomorrow's necktie.

Then he did go to the door, all the way this time.

And he turned and looked at her so tenderly, so softly, that the look was a caress in itself. With just a touch of rue in it.

"Are you afraid?" he said.

"You mean now, about your going downstairs awhile?"

"No, I mean after—when I come back again."

She dropped her eyes only momentarily. Then she quickly raised them again, and they looked directly into his, candidly and confidently. "No, because I know you love me. And even if part of love is strange, if the rest of it is good, then all of it has to be good. And soon there *are* no different parts to it, it is all just one love. Those are the words my mother told me, when she kissed me good-bye."

"I love you," he said, as devoutly as when you're in a church saying a prayer meant only for God and yourself to hear. "So don't be afraid." Then he said only one thing more. "I'll be back in just a little bit."

Then he closed the door. But for a minute or two his face seemed to glow there where it had been. Then it slowly wore thin, and the light it had made went away.

Like the illusion of love itself does.

In a prim little flurry now she started disrobing. Intent on having it complete before she should be interrupted.

At the moment of passing from chemise to nightrobe, quite instinc-

tively and without knowing she did it, she briefly closed her eyes. Then as the gown rippled downward to the floor, she opened them again. It was not, she had learned or been cautioned when still quite a little girl, nice to scrutinize your own body when it was unclothed. The gown was batiste, a trousseau gown, with eyelet embroidery and a bertha—that is to say, an ample cape-like flap covering both shoulders; it was bluish in the shadows where it fell hollowed, pink where her body touched against it, but its actual color was snowy-white.

She had always brushed her hair before retiring. She did it now, for there was something comforting about the sense of normalcy it gave to do it; it was like something familiar to cling to in an eddy of imminent strangeness. She counted each stroke to herself, up to fifty; she longed to go past there, up to a hundred, for it would have seemed to help to arrest time, not allow it to go forward, but she conscientiously curbed herself and refrained.

Then she gave a look around the room, inquiringly and still with that flurried intensity. There was nothing left to do now, no remaining detail unattended.

She went to the bed, turned her back to it, and entered it.

She drew the covers up tightly about one shoulder—the other was turned inward to the pillow.

She gave a little sigh, of finality, of satisfaction, of when there is utterly nothing left to do and one is content there isn't.

Her eyes remained fixed on the door. Not in a hard stare, but in soft expectancy. Nothing tenderer in this world, the eyes of youth looking for its love.

Perhaps he was standing just outside the door, uncertain whether to come in. Perhaps young men had trepidations at such a delicate time as this, just as she—just as girls—did. Perhaps if she were to go to the door, open it, that would resolve his irresolution for him....

At last, pinning her underlip beneath her teeth as if to steel herself to the act, she emerged from the bed once more. Because this was a door, and outside was a public corridor, she put on her wrapper first and gathered it tight.

♥ The EVILS of ILLICIT SEX RELATIONS ♥

When Such Reward Is Offered For Vice

And Want And Threatened Starvation Held Out To Virtue

It is a physiological fact long demonstrated that persons possessing a loving disposition borrow less of the cares of life, and also live much longer, than persons with a strong, narrow and selfish nature.

Love strengthens health and disappointment cultivates disease. A person in love will invariably enjoy the best of health. Ninety-nine per cent of our strong-constitutioned men, now in physical ruin, have wrecked themselves on the breakers of an unnatural love. Nothing but right love and right marriage will restore them to health.

Nothing tears the life out of man more than lust, vulgar thoughts and immoral conduct. The libertine or harlot has changed love, God's purest gift to man, into lust. They cannot acquire love in its purity again, the sacred flame has vanished forever. Love is pure and cannot be found in the heart of a seducer.

A woman is never so bright and full of health as when deeply in love. Many sickly and frail women are snatched from the clutches of some deadly diseases and restored to health by falling in love.

It is a long established fact that married persons are healthier than unmarried persons, thus it proves that health and happiness belong to the home. Health depends on the mind. Love places the mind into a delightful state and quickens every human function, makes the blood circulate and weaves threads of joy into cables of domestic love.

Love makes people look younger in years. People in unhappy homes look older and more worn and fatigued. A woman at thirty, well mated, looks five or ten years younger than a woman of the same age unhappily married. Old maids and bachelors always look older than they are. A flirting widow always looks younger than an old maid of the same age.

Without love there would be no organized households, and consequently, none of that earnest endeavor for competence and respectability, which is the mainspring of human effort; none of those sweet softening, restraining and elevating influences of domestic life, which can alone fill the earth with the glory of the Lord and make glad the city of Zion.

1. Her mother refuses to satisfy her perfectly natural curiosity about the mystery of life.

2. Her education is thus delayed until she is sent away to boarding school.

3. Her knowledge of life increases step by step—faster than she realizes.

4. She discovers that there is a law which no reputable physician will break.

5. In desperation she decides to risk her life, rather than to face the consequences of her ignorance.

6. Her education is complete.

⌐Hotel Room⌐

Then she went over to it, the door, and stood there by it, summoning up fresh reserves of courage, sorely needed. She put her hand out gingerly toward the knob, the way you reach for something very hot that you're afraid will burn you.

Then she hesitated there like that, hand on knob.

If he didn't discover her in the act of doing this, she wouldn't tell him—later—that she had done it. It smacked a little too much of boldness, or, what was equally as bad, impatience.

Now she touched the door with her other hand, and inclined her head closer toward it, as if trying not so much to listen but rather to divine by some other subtle sense whether he was present there on the other side of it—or not.

She opened the door and looked, and he wasn't; it was empty there on the other side.

She sighed, and the attentive forward-lean her body had taken relapsed into a backward inert slump of disappointment.

Perhaps he was further down the corridor, walking to and—? She tightened further her already tightened wrapper, and like an aerialist walking on a single wire, advanced through the door-opening and out to the corridor proper, one foot keeping in a straight line behind the other.

It was empty from end to end. Just carpeting, and light bulbs looking so lonely against the wall, like forgotten little orphan suns. She remembered the hall from before, from when they'd first come in, but it hadn't looked so lonely then. Maybe because she hadn't been so lonely then either.

She stood there long, long moments. But nothing, no one, came into sight. The emptiness stayed as empty as before. She re-entered the room at last, closed the door, and mournfully inclined her head against it on the inside in a desolate sort of way. Then that ended too, presently, as all attitudes and postures must sooner or later.

She moved away from there and roamed the room, without a destination, deep in thought, absently touching things as she went, to guide herself. He could not mean to stay away this

long. He had lost track of the time. That must be it. That must be the explanation, there could be no other.

Perhaps if she called down, he would understand. Yes, but what genteel way was there to convey the message? "Would you ask my husband to come up, please?" She shuddered at that. It was so unthinkable it made her squeeze her eyes tightly shut for a moment. No, she couldn't say anything like that. The man at the phone—

A man's voice, frighteningly immediate and immediately frightening, the gruffest voice a man had ever used in the whole world before, the harshest, the raspiest, said: "Yes, please? Can I be of service?'"

She began too low, and had to start over at once.

"Beg pardon?"

"I said, I can't seem to open one of our suitcases. My husband—" She swallowed hard, and almost spoiled it, but recovered in time. "Would you ask him if he has the key with him, please?"

"I will without fail, madam, just as soon as I see him."

She'd had the same sensation once years before, when a small boy in a tree had dropped a soft splashy snowball on her as she passed below and it had struck and disintegrated at the nape of her neck.

"Oh, isn't he—? I thought he was—"

"He went out of the building, madam. I saw him as he went past."

"But are you sure it was—?"

"The night bellboy told me it was the young man from '23."

She didn't speak any further. She hadn't strength enough to hang up, she hadn't fortitude enough to continue listening.

He must have sensed an urgency she hadn't wanted to show. "Shall I send out and see if he's outside by the entrance?"

She didn't say anything. Her breath was too much in the way, rising up again before it had even finished going down, leaving no passage clear.

The wait was cruel and long. And this had nothing to do with measured time, for even had it been of no duration whatever, an immediate turnabout, it would have been no less cruel, no less long. The heart cannot

● The DIFFERENCES BETWEEN MEN and WOMEN ●

Man is the creature of interest and ambition. His nature leads him forth into the struggle and bustle of the world. He seeks for fame, for fortune and dominion over his fellow men. But a woman's whole life is the history of the affections. The heart is her world, it is there her ambition strives for empire, it is there her ambition seeks for hidden treasures. She sends forth her sympathies of adventure, she embarks her whole soul in the traffic of affection; and if shipwrecked her case is hopeless, for it is bankruptcy of the heart.

♥ WOMAN'S LOVE ♥

Woman's love is stronger than death, it rises superior to adversity, and towers in sublime beauty above the niggardly selfishness of the world. Misfortune cannot suppress it, enmity cannot alienate it, temptation cannot enslave it. It ever remains the same to sweeten existence, to purify the cup of life on the rugged pathway to the grave, and melt to moral pliability the brittle nature of man.

1. He decides to verify some of the
stories he has heard.

2. After three weeks of treatment (?)
and the payment of $50.00, he is
pronounced cured.

3. He decides to settle down.

4. His wife becomes the pitiful victim
of his ignorance.

5. He learns with horror that he had
never been cured.

6. Who is to blame for their childless
and unhappy married life?

◁ Hotel Room ▷

measure, it can only feel; in a single instant it can feel as much as in a long slow hour, it cannot feel more than that.

There was a background murmur soon, as of tidings being brought, and then a clear-spoken address directly to her: "He doesn't seem to be out there right now, madam. He may have taken a short stroll away from the hotel. Just as soon as he returns I'll notify him that you—"

She heard him go, at the other end, and what was there to stay for anyway? But she stayed; just stayed there, on and on, through long slow minutes that never seemed to pass away.

The night wore on, with a hush like funeral velvet draperies.

"Don't let the day come. Don't let it come yet. Wait till he's back first. Then let it come."

But mercilessly the night thinned away, as if there were a giant unseen blackboard eraser at work, rubbing it out. And in the new light he didn't come, just as he hadn't in the former dark. Still her eyes stared out over the woolen folds, looking nowhere, seeing nothing now. Duller than dull, hopelessly opaque.

She must have slept, or dozed awake at least. Her head went over a little to the side at last, became more inert. The eyes never fully closed, but lost some of their haunted fixity. The lids did not drop over them the whole way, but sagged to a somnolent meridian.

The fidgeting of the knob must have been hours after. No hope came with its fluttering, somehow. Hope would not come back; it had been dead too long perhaps. It didn't even stir, strangely enough. Nor when the questioning tap came. Nor when it parted at the seams and a gap was made, empty the first few instants. Then an errant flounce of skirt peered momentarily, showing hope it had been right to lie there dead.

Above, a head looked cautiously in, everything else kept back.

The woman was in maid's headgarb, ruched cap atop a massive pillow of upturned red hair, kept walled in by barrettes. She was buxom, florid, maternal in every respect. Save perhaps

the actuality.

"Did I come too soon, now?" she murmured softly.

The eyes just looked at her.

"They told me one of the rooms around here was a bride and groom, but sure it's the first day for all of us, and I would be getting mixed up like this."

The eyes just looked.

"Shall I step out and be coming back a little later then?"

A voice like the echo of far-off sound said: "It doesn't matter."

"Did the young man step out for a minute?"

The far-off voice said: "He's gone."

She advanced more fully into the room now, concerned. "What's the matter, darlin'? What ails—?"

The bunched-up robe suddenly exploded like an overstuffed pod, lay there flaccid, the chair was empty, and she was clinging to her, and being clung to. Someone of one's own kind, another woman. Someone like your mother, someone like your sister. Someone like—you.

The maid held her, and patted her, and coaxed her. "Sh, darlin'. Sure and he'll be back before you know it. Any minute now, through the door he'll be coming."

"He won't. He won't. He never will again."

"How lang ago did he leave? How lang is it he's gone?"

"At twelve. I think it was at twelve. But I don't know any more. I can't remember any more."

"But sure, darlin', it's only a little after two o'clock now."

"At twelve last night."

The ruddy face whitened. For a moment *her* eyes were frightened too, then she covered it up. She patted the girl some more, she held her to her. Then she left her briefly, saying she'd be back. The girl just stood there exactly where she'd left her, like someone deprived of her own powers of locomotion....

The girl remained alone.

Some time after, a knock again interrupted her solitude. The knock did not wait for a response, but the door was opened immediately on its heels, and a dignified and well-dressed gentleman entered, with the air of someone who did not need to ask per-

♦ IF EVERY MAN WERE STRAIGHT ♦

If every man were straight there would be no such thing as prostitution. There would be no loose women if there were no loose men. True love would find a place in every man's life. He would respect and honor all women and would love one woman supremely. There would be no venereal diseases. (Only the lowest, most contemptible brute would marry, knowing that his venereal disease was still acute) and there would be fewer childless homes, as gonorrhea causes sterility in both men and women.

♦ ETHICS OF THE UNMARRIED ♦

SPOONING. One of the very first problems that confront the guiding light in a young man's life is this. "Is there any harm in spooning?" We mean by "spooning" the kissing, fondling and reclining in each other's lap which seems to be a very common means of entertainment among the young people of today. What harm can there be, you ask, in a simple kiss or other form of endearment between a young man and his fiancée? What possible danger can there be in letting young folks be young folks? Our answer is that while the harm may not be apparent in the act itself, it is the after effects we must look for.

THE RESULTS OF SPOONING. The Bible tells you the results of spooning. "Thou shalt not commit adultery" was one of the fundamentals of the Mosaic Law. This applied only to the act itself. Jesus Christ gave the proper interpretation of the law when he said: "Whosoever looketh on a woman to lust after her hath committed adultery with her already in his heart." Spooning has a very definite and a very harmful physical effect upon the body. The after effects are in all probability far worse than the effects of actual adultery. Many a young man has gone to the altar temporarily impotent as a result of a long intimate courtship. Nervousness, invalidism, and various ovarian troubles are among common results of over stimulated sexual apparatus in young women given to too much spooning. It is safe to say that numberless unhappy marriages can be traced to the sexual disorders brought on or aggravated by familiarities before marriage. God alone know how many girls and boys have contracted a serious venereal disease as a result of what they considered a little harmless diversion.

◁ Hotel Room ▷

mission but was free to enter a room like this at any time he chose.

He was about her father's age, and dressed somewhat as she had seen her father dressed; but not at ordinary times, only on rare occasions, such as churchgoing on an Easter Sunday morning. He had a very heavy down-turned mustache, glistening with wax, and wore a small flower, she did not know its name, in the buttonhole of his swallowtail coat.

"My poor child," was his greeting to her. "I've come to see what can be done about this." Then, after having already seated himself, he asked, "May I sit down a moment and have a little chat with you?"

Her face flickered briefly as the sympathy in his voice revived her grief. She nodded mutely; he made her feel less lost and lonesome.

"I'm Mr. Lindsey, dear," he introduced himself; and though he didn't add that he was the manager, somehow she know that he must be. He had too much of an air of habitual authority about him.

"Tell me about yourself," he said artlessly.

And, hesitantly and awkwardly at first, but soon without any self-consciousness whatever or even aware-ness that she was doing so, she was answering the sprinkling of guiding questions that he put to shape the course of her talk. She did not even know that they were questions, they were so deftly inserted. She did not even know, in telling him about their house at home, that she had told him what street it was on, or what its number was, or of course what town it was situated in. Sitting back at ease in his chair, one knee crossed above the other, nodding benignly, he skillfully slanted the conversation.

Then almost in mid-word—hers, not his own—his knees had uncou-pled, he was on his feet taking leave of her, and the refreshing little flow of confidence had ended. Mouth still open on an unfinished sentence, she watched him go to the door and open it, with a soothing "Forgive me, my child; I must hurry. There's an awful lot to do here today."

"Good-bye, Mr. Lindsey," she said

forlornly, eyes hopeful to the end that he might change his mind and remain.

Just as he closed the door she heard him say, in a tactfully lowered voice to someone who must have remained out there waiting for him: "They must be sent for. She can't remain here alone like this."

When the haze that had misted her eyes had cleared away again, as at last it did, Papa was there in the room with her; he was the first one she saw. He was standing, back from the bed a lit-tle, beside a chair. In the chair sat Mamma, pressed close against him, his arm consolingly about her shoulder. Within her clenched hand, raised to just below her face, she held a tiny balled-up handkerchief, and from time to time would press it to her nose. But she was not crying now, though just previously she evidently had been. This was just the leftover corrective from when she had been crying. Both their faces were haunted with concern, their eyes were fixed troubledly on her, with a steadfastness which indi-cated they had been gazing at her like this for a long time past. They did not smile at her, seemed too deeply trou-bled to be able to, even when they saw that she recognized them. Papa's mus-tache even seemed to droop, for it was so heavy that it took whatever shape his mouth took under it, and his mouth therefore must have been turned deeply down.

Nearer at hand was someone else. She only noticed him last, for his head had been bent down low, listening to her breathing. She knew him to be a doctor, for she felt the tiny coolness his instrument made, moving here and there about her chest. She wasn't afraid; she had had doctors do this before with a stethoscope, for a bad cold in the chest, perhaps. This was *home*, a part of home; a part of being with Papa and Mamma, a part of being safe, of being cared for....

He put away his stethoscope, and turned to them, to Mamma and Papa, and said, "She is sound physically. There is no need for worry on that score. But—" And then he didn't finish it.

Mamma's face tightened up even more than it was already. "What is it, Doctor?" she said in a whisper that was almost superstitiously fearful.

THE CAUSES OF SPOONING. 1. Almost all young children are teased about sweethearts. Instead of trying to develop lofty ideals of modesty, kissing between boys and girls of a tender age is actually encouraged by older people who should know better. Hands off now, henceforth and forever more should be our slogan.

2. Another cause for spooning is to be found in the false ideas of love which are indelibly impressed on the youthful mind by cheap literature and musical comedies (so called) whose vulgarity and sensualism are allowed to exist unmolested without any thought of their consequences.

3. Certain unscrupulous individuals grow rich through the manufacture and distribution of suggestive postcards, obscene stereoptican views, and inexcusable books, and type written pamphlets. They willfully exaggerate the pleasures of vice and excite a prurient curiosity about all such things.

4. The spirit of boastfulness is a real cause of the prevalence of spooning. A boy gets the idea from his misinformed companions that kissing and hugging a girl is something to be bragged about.

5. And finally, the modern dance must take its share of the blame. The Tango, the Texas Tommy, the One Step and Walking the Dog had their very origins in the palaces of lust on the Barbary Coast of San Francisco. It was only a step from the house of ill fame, to the public cafe, to the private dance, and thence to the home itself. These dances are as unrefined as their names.

WHICH SHALL I TAKE?

A Career, a Life of Pleasure or Motherhood?

THE REAL FUNCTION OF SPOONING AND WHAT IS LOVE? How is it possible to distinguish between true love and a sex thrill? It is safe to say that true love and sensual love, side by side, cannot long endure. A young man who kisses, hugs, and fondles a girl, and a young girl who is permitting these intimacies, are unable to distinguish the difference between that sensual thrill of sex so quickly banished by satiety and the mutual respect and admiration which endures. How frequently the discovery comes too late.

⌐Hotel Room¬

"She has suffered great shock," he said, and he rose now to finally face them in entirety, so that she could see only his back. He crossed the room before speaking further, and then, trickling water into a tumbler, said, "And those things sometimes take long to wear off." Then bringing the tumbler back to her side, he took from his bag which sat open on the floor a neat little oblong paper packet, and deftly unfolded it to make a little trough of it, and from this allowed a white powder to sift into the water and cloud it to the hue of diluted milk. "And sometimes never," he said, concluding at last his sentence.

Mamma gave a start and cried, "Oh, Doctor— Oh, no—!"

He stirred the dose by hand-motion alone, without the aid of any spoon, by giving his wrist a rotary motion. Then passed it to her and said, "Drink this, dear. Right down."

She knew the taste, she'd experienced it before. Calomel.

"Now lie back and rest," he said, when he'd taken the empty tumbler back from her, and gently placed his hand upon her forehead, again more as a gesture of what he wanted her to do than by exerting any actual pressure upon her.

She lay back and watched and listened, while he gave them his undivided attention at last.

Mamma said pleadingly, "What shall we do, Doctor? Doctor, what shall we do?"

"There is nothing you *can* do, except wait and see. Nothing I can do, nothing anyone can do. Except let time go by."

"Shall we take her back with us now, Doctor?" Mamma asked.

"Is it far?" he said.

She told him where it was, in Indiana. He closed his eyes briefly, as though he would have preferred it to be not that far. Then he said, "Yes, it's better if you do, even if the trip is a tiring one. The sooner you take her out of this terrible room and what it spells for her, the better off she'll be"....

The doctor took up his hat, and went to shake hands with Papa. Mamma quickly let the drawer be momentarily, to go and join in the leave-taking.

Someone knocked on the door, and the doctor went to it and looked out. He stood there awhile, just his back showing, while someone spoke to him.

When he had closed the door again, he motioned them to come nearer. "They've found him," he breathed.

"Is he—?" Papa whispered.

"They found his body," the doctor said. "The pockets were all inside out. He didn't have his wallet with him. Maybe if he had had it on him, he wouldn't have been killed."

Mamma wrung her hands.

Papa looked down at the floor.

"I leave it up to you whether to tell her or not," the doctor said. He sighed and shook his head. "Keep her to yourselves a lot. All you can. Don't let people hurt her."

Mamma said, "Who would want to hurt her, Doctor? Our little girl."

"Nobody will want to. But everyone will. Every time she sees a boy holding a girl by the hand. Every time she sees a couple dancing. Every time she sees a baby roll by in its carriage— Keep her to yourselves a lot. All you can, all you can."

A porter came in and took the valises out, but she was only dimly aware of that, for Mamma was standing before her blocking her view.

Mamma put her hat on for her last of all, and adjusted it, and thrust the pins through it. The hat that went way up on one side, way down on the other.

Then Mamma placed an arm about her waist, and kissed her once again on the forehead, the kiss that she remembered so well from her childhood, the kiss of security, the kiss of consolation, the kiss of belonging to someone, of being a part of them; the kiss of home. And Mamma murmured gently beside her ear, "Come, our little girl is coming home with us."

Step by step, with her arm about her, she led her over to the door, then out past it to where Papa stood waiting, and reaching behind her, started to draw it tactfully closed after them.

But just as it was closing, the girl herself gave an abrupt turn, and pleading, "Just one moment—! Only one —!" stepped back to it and looked in once more, while Mamma's arm still held her around the waist.

• *The* POWER AND PECULIARITIES *of* LOVE •

We all know the evils which attend the young man or the young woman who falls by the wayside. It is unnecessary to go into detail. We live in a civilization which has adopted certain definite standards of morality; we have laws to protect the sanctity of the home. The man or woman who breaks these laws runs the risk of a four fold penalty: social ostracism, legal punishment, loathsome disease, and the wrath of God.

Early marriage seems to be the only workable solution to circumvent the evils of illicit sex relations. Preach the gospel of early marriage and it will save the day.

A young woman who is not willing to assume the responsibility of a true wife, and be crowned with the sacred diadem of motherhood, should never think of getting married. We have too many young ladies today who despise maternity, who openly vow that they will never be burdened with children, and yet enter matrimony at the first opportunity. What is the result? Unless a young lady believes that motherhood is noble, is honorable, is divine, and is willing to carry out that sacred function of her nature, she had a thousand times better refuse every proposal and enter some honorable occupation.

The "Bridal Tour" is considered by many newly married couples as a necessary introduction to a life of connubial joy. The period immediately following should be one of rest.

However, the money expended on the wedding ceremony and the tour of the principal cities, might, in most cases, be applied to a multitude of after-life comforts of far more lasting value and importance. To be sure it is not pleasant for the bride, should she remain at home, to pass through the ordeal of criticism and vulgar comments of acquaintances and friends, and hence, to escape this, the young couple may feel like getting away for a time.

If the conventional tour is taken, the husband should remember that his bride cannot stand the same amount of tramping around and sightseeing that he can. The female organs of generation are so easily affected by excessive exercise of the limbs which support them, that at this critical period it would be a foolish and costly experience to drag a lady hurriedly around the country on an extensive and protracted round of sightseeing or visiting. Unless good common sense is displayed in the manner of spending the "honeymoon" it will prove very untrue to its name.

ᴥ Hotel Room ᴦ

And staring around at the emptiness, as if seeking him everywhere and finding him nowhere, she called out with whispered intensity: "Good-bye, Johnny! Good-bye! And good-bye to me too. For we both died in here the other night."

The Night of September 30th, 1957

She arrived at about nine, that last night. That last night of the hotel. She came alone in a taxi. It had to take its place in what almost amounted to a conveyor-belt of taxis, each stopping in turn at the entrance, then drawing away again. There was this difference: hers was bringing its fare to the hotel, the rest were all taking theirs from it.

She was very frail and very old, and looked very small the way she sat there in the exact center of the broad rear seat. Her face looked unlined and peaceful, as though care had passed over it lightly.

The driver stopped at the entrance, his car grazing the one ahead as it drew away, the one just in back grazing his as it closed in to wait its turn.

She leaned forward a trifle and asked, "Is it that now?"

He looked at his watch and said, "Yes, ma'am, exactly that."

She nodded, gratified. "I wanted it to be that exactly."

"It's a hard thing to do," he said. "Let you out somewhere at an exact certain minute. I had to take you around the block three times. That made the meter climb up."

"I don't mind," she reassured him quickly. "I don't care." She paid him, and then when he turned in the seat to try and pass the change back to her, she put the flat of her hand up against it. "No, I don't want anything back," she said.

"But that was a five," he said.

"I know it was," she said imperturbably. "My sight is good." Then she added, as though that explained her generosity, "I don't ride in taxis very often."

He got out and opened the rear door for her and helped her down. She looked smaller than ever standing beside him there on the sidewalk and with two tremendous walls of baggage towering on both sides of her. He got

her bag out. She only had one, a very small one, lightweight and old-fashioned. It too looked small, just as she did.

"The place is coming down, you know," he told her.

"I know it is," she said. "I can read the papers." But it wasn't said with asperity.

"They're putting up a twenty-six-story office building on the site."

"Twenty-eight," she corrected him. Then she gave a contemptuous sniff, presumably intended for office buildings in general and not just the difference of two floors.

She left him and went inside, carrying the bag herself. She stopped at the desk. "I have a reservation for Room 923," she said. "I engaged it several weeks ago."

He scanned some sort of a chart he had tacked up there off to one side. "I believe that floor's already been closed off," he said. "Won't one of the lower floors do?"

She was firm. "No. I specified that room, and my reservation was accepted. I had it confirmed. I won't take any other."

He went off and spoke to somebody about it. Then he came back and said, "You can have that room." He presented the register to her for her signature. It was open very far to the back, at the last few of its pages. She fingered the thick bulk of its preceding ones.

"How far back does this go?" she asked him.

He had to look at the opening page to find out. "Nineteen forty."

"And what happened to the old ones? There must have been others before this. What happened to the very first one of all?"

"I haven't the faintest idea," he admitted. "Probably done away with long ago. Thrown out."

"Thrown out!" she said with severity. "Things like that shouldn't be thrown out." She shook her head with disapproval. "Very well, I'll sign," she said. She wrote "Mrs. John Compton" in a wavering spidery hand, almost ghostly compared to some of the firm, fullbodied signatures that had gone before it.

He had to keep palming the bell repeatedly before he could attract any attention. The staff had already been

THE CONSUMMATION OF MARRIAGE. *The first time that the husband and wife cohabit together after the ceremony has been performed is called the consummation of marriage. Many grave errors have been committed by people in this, when one or both of the contracting parties were not physically or sexually in a condition to carry out the marriage relation. A marriage is not complete without this in the eyes of the law. In most states of the U.S. marriage is legally declared void and of no effect where it is not possible to consummate the marriage relation.*

Let every man remember that the legal right of marriage does not carry with it the moral right to injure for life the loving companion he has chosen. Ignorance may be the cause, but every man, before he marries should know something of physiology and the laws of health.

SENSUALITY. *Lust crucifies love. The young sensual husband is generally at fault. Passion sways and the duty to the bride and wife is not thought of, and so a modest young wife is often forced and assaulted by the unsympathetic haste of her husband. An amorous man in that way soon destroys his own love, and thus is laid the foundation for many difficulties that soon develop into trouble and disturb the happiness of both.*

For more than one night it will be wise, indeed, if the wife's confidence shall be as much wooed and won by patient, delicate and prolonged courting, as before the marriage engagement. How long should this period of waiting be can only be decided by the circumstance of any case. The bride will ultimately deny no favor which is sought with full deference to her modesty, and in connection with, bestiality is not exhibited. Her nature is that of delicacy; her affection is of a refined character, if the love and conduct offered to her are a careful effort to adapt roughness and strength to her refinement and weakness, her admiration and responsive love will be excited to the utmost.

Sexual excesses often lead to the rapid development of some disease or ailment. For instance, if a man has weak lungs, the exhaustion caused by his intemperance may bring on consumption. The same thing is true of tendencies toward other diseases. Sexual excess weakens the vitality and lessens the resistance. It is responsible for many female disorders.

THE RESULT. *Sexual excess always brings punishment, either in ill health, in impotence or in lost love. The sexual question undoubtedly is the underlying cause of more friction and unhappiness in married life, than any other thing. Outraged sexuality causes antagonism and hatred which actually exceed in intensity the former feelings of love and respect.*

◁Hotel Room▷

skeletonized. Finally a harried bellboy appeared, picked up her bag, and mechanically started toward the street entrance with it. A sharp clang of the bell brought him around in his tracks.

"Show this lady to 923."

The bellboy showed undisguised astonishment for a minute. "You mean the lady's coming *in? Now?*"

"The lady's checking in, not out."

As she closed the door and turned away from it, she said: "This is a room of happiness. This is a room of reunion."

She began to unpack her bag now. From it she took a wafer-flat oblong white cardboard box, fastened with white paper tape.

"He didn't even want to put it in a box for me. I *told* him it was for a gift," she complained aloud, as if at the memory of some recent disputation. "Nowadays everything's too much for them."

She removed the bow-tied tape and the lid, peeled open the two interlocking leaves of crisp tissue paper, and took out a necktie, bright and new. She went to the dresser top with it and laid it down there, painstakingly choosing a certain exact spot to place it in, measuring it off almost, moving it a little, smoothing it a little, until she had attained the desired accuracy of position.

"Johnny, this is for you. For you to wear tomorrow. They lost your other one, that night. And I don't want my Johnny to be without a necktie."

Then she lowered her face, touched her lips to it, and said with old-fashioned formality, "Wear it in good health, dear."

She returned to the bag, and as she took from it still something else, turned her head once more toward the dresser, as if addressing an after-remark to someone standing there unseen. "Luckily I didn't have to buy you one of these. I don't know much about picking them out." She opened a packet of yellowed tissue and from it took a wallet, worn with much handling and giving at the seams. "I've kept it for you all these years. Just the way it was. Thirty-nine dollars and eighty-five cents. Perhaps the money will come in handy to you. You might

want us to go sightseeing tomorrow, on our first day together."

She placed it close to the tie, in just a certain place upon the dresser, and adjusted it too as she had the tie, as if fitting it to some invisible guide lines.

Returning to the opened bag a third and final time, she took out a neatly folded nightgown, and holding it up at shoulder-height, allowed it to fall open of its own weight. It was old-fashioned yet not old-fashioned, for fashion had come full circle again and its voluminous width and full-length sleeves were newer than the scantiness of intervening decades. It was old rather than old-fashioned, of finest batiste, with eyelet embroidery and a bertha, all handwork, the way a bridal gown should be, but citron-color with long existence. And the ghosts of hundreds of successive little bags of sachet still clung to it, even though they were gone now.

She disrobed now and put it on. It took on bluish hollows where it fell away from her body, yellow opacity where it clung close. It detracted from her age. She did not look like a young girl in it. Not even like a young woman. She looked like a wizened child, parading around in one of its elder's garments.

She loosened and brushed her hair now, with a brush that came from the bag. And that done, she went to the light switch and darkened the room. Then she went to the bed and got into it, but not with a complete absence of any effort. Lying there, she stirred awhile until she had attained the desired comfort, and then lay there awhile longer after that, in repose, murmuring to herself. Aloud but softly. Just over her breath, as when one says a prayer.

"Good night, my Johnny. Good night, my love. We'll see each other tomorrow. And tomorrow *will* come. Oh, I know it will. I've never doubted that it will for a single moment.

"And thank you for so many things. So many, many things. As I've thanked you for them so many times before. Thank you for a perfect marriage. The most perfect a mariage could be. Never an angry word, never a sullen silence; never a quarrel, never a jealous stab, never a drunken stumble. Never the fright of illness, nor the

TELL ME SWEETHEART NOW I PRAY
WHEN WILL BE OUR WEDDING DAY?

♥ HOW MUCH MAKES IT WORTH IT? ♥

If delicate ladies had to risk immodest bestiality from their ignorant new husbands, as well as loss of love and loathsome disease, there had to be a payoff for that horrendous wedding night somewhere. Though of course the big payoff was not having to go through life as a pitiful old maid, those who needed immediate gratification found it in the trousseau. If Mommy and Daddy came through, this was the bounty reaped: two pairs of shoes, one pair of slippers, one pair of boots, one parasol, three bonnets, two corsets, two frocks, three chemises, two evening dresses, two blouses, two skirts, one bathing suit, four slips, three petticoats, five pairs of lace undies, twelve ribbons of velvet and satin, one long coat, one short coat, one shawl or fur wrap, three pairs of gloves, two necklaces, one bracelet, and a present of whatever family heirloom happened to be lying around.

CORNELL'S BENZOIN COSMETIC SOAP TRADE MARK.

ASK FOR THE "GLOVE THUMB"

"Retrograde" Seamed Mitts.
THE VERY BEST MADE.   Kept by all Large Dealers.

THE CROWN PERFUMERY C EXTRA CONCENTRATED Crab-Apple BLOSSOMS. 177 NEW BOND ST LONDON

A New and really useful Wedding present

THE BEST CORSET SUBSTITUTES.

COMPROMISE BODICE   JENNESS MILLER MODEL BODICE   EQUIPOISE WAIST

Under the same old moon.

⊲Hotel Room⊳

ignominy of nursing and watching some of its more ignoble symptoms. Never the strife of lack of earning power, nor the bitter recriminations of failure and mistake and final ill-fortune. And above all, for not slowly aging before my eyes, as I would have slowly aged before yours, until finally neither of us was what the other had married, but somebody else entirely. Some unknown old man. Some unknown old woman. Thank you for staying young. And for letting me stay young along with you. A lifetime of youth. Eternal spring. Thank you for always being the bridegroom of our first night, romance blazing in your eyes. Thank you for all this. For all this, thank you forevermore. Good night, my beloved, my only, only love, my lifetime's love. Good night—the word I like to call you best of all: my husband. Your wife is wishing you good night."

In the morning, after her first discovery, the maid came back in a few minutes bringing the manager with her this time. They both looked at her, first, from where they stood. Then the manager went over closer to her and gently touched her forehead.

He turned around and said, "She's gone."

"I knew she was," the maid whispered. "I could tell even from the doorway."

He came back to where the maid was standing and they both continued to look at her from there, the serene figure in the bed.

"That smile," he said under his breath. "Did you ever see anyone look so perfectly at rest, with such a peaceful, contented smile on their face?"

"She looks so happy," the maid concurred. "More like a—like a new bride than an old lady whose time has come to die."

"I guess she was once," he mused. "Just like this room was brand-new once. And then they both got older—the two of them—slowly, slowly, over the years. A little bit at a time, and then they got—like they both are now. Done with. People are a lot like hotel rooms, when you come to think of it."

A Confusing Honeymoon: Goh Kong Tai and Miss Hong (left) and Miss Eng after their wedding ceremony in Singapore, where polygamy is legal.

CHAPTER FOUR

A HONEYMOON BELIEVE IT OR NOT

A Compendium of Bizarre Honeymoon Rites Around the World

Birds do it, bees do it,
Even educated fleas do it.
Let's do it, let's fall in love.
In Spain, the best upper sets do it,
Lithuanians and Letts do it,
Let's do it, let's fall in love.

The Dutch in old Amsterdam do it,
Not to mention the Finns,
Folks in Siam do it,
Think of Siamese twins.

Some Argentines, without means, do it,
People say, in Boston, even beans do it,
Let's do it, let's fall in love.

Sponges, they say, do it,
Oysters, down in Oyster Bay, do it,
Let's do it, let's fall in love.
Cold Cape Cod clams, 'gainst their wish, do it,
Even lazy jelly fish do it,
Let's do it, let's fall in love.

Electric eels, I might add, do it,
Though it shocks 'em I know.
Why ask if shad do it,
Waiter, bring me shad roe.

In shallow shoals, English soles do it,
Goldfish, in the privacy of bowls, do it,
Let's do it, let's fall in love.

LET'S DO IT. Words and Music by Cole Porter.

Among the Bantu Kavirondo tribes in East Africa, the bride and bridegroom are required to consummate their marriage in front of a large group of young girls and women. They do this to give publicity to the legality of their marriage, and it is believed that the women will spread the word faster than the men. The amount of giggling and embarrassment expressed by the witnesses is an indication of the success of the marriage consummation and of the husband's prowess and virility.

♥

In Germany, it has been customary for the husband to consummate the marriage wearing socks or some other form of leggings to keep disease and evil spirits from his new wife's bed. It has also been expected that the husband would undergo a lengthy foot bath before taking his marriage vows.

A Gadaba girl of thirteen marries a Gadaba boy of eight, India.

The decoration of a Batak bride in Indonesia.

Teutonic and Slavonic countries had the custom of making sure that the bride and bridegroom spent their wedding night under the same blanket. Actual intercourse was not necessary to ensure consummation. Teutonic witnesses saw to it that the bride and bridegroom were physically touching under the same blanket, and that there was no fakery in the sheeting of the bed.

♥

An old French peasant custom allowed that the father of the bride lay a long loaf of bread in the marriage bed to ensure fertility in the bride and virility in the groom. The success or failure of the wedding night was determined by the condition of the bread the following morning. A crumpled loaf, and an excess of crumbs, indicated great marital success.

♥

Among the Nandi of British East Africa, the honeymooning couple is bound and braided together with reeds of grass which they proceed to rip apart and destroy during their marriage consummation. A similar custom is found in the Basuto tribe, who substitute a strip of the dewlap of a slaughtered ox. It is tied around the couple's waists and is also expected to be broken during intercourse.

♥

It is an old Swedish custom that a small boy sleep on the bride's side of the bed on her wedding night, ensuring that her first offspring shall be male.

♥

Among the Oriental Jews, it was customary for the bride's parents to place a large raw fish in the marriage bed as a fertility symbol and aphrodisiac.

♥

In Algeria, the bridegroom casts raw eggs at his bedded bride during their marriage consummation. The messy pelting ensures her fertility and ease in her subsequent childbirth.

Two ushers, who happen to be the bride's brothers, lead the procession at a Serbian peasant wedding.

Brides among the Brahmans of Eastern Bengal demand that their husbands sleep with a large padlock on their lips, so that as the bride slowly turns the key, she shows that "the door to unkind speech has been closed."

♥

A complicated Moroccan custom: The bride mounts a ram which is to be slaughtered, and boxes its ears. The ram is representative of the bride's new husband. When the ram is slaughtered, its stomach is removed. The bride proceeds to put her right foot into the dead ram's stomach. She then removes her now bloody slipper and, standing at the door of her honeymoon chamber, waves it back and forth seven times. She enters the chamber, and lies in waiting for her new husband. When the groom enters the chamber, she ambushes him, and beats him with the blood-drenched slipper. If the husband cries out, then she will be the ruler in the marriage.

♥

Among the Eskimos of North America, it is a common rite that the bridesmaids and the bride warm up the bed for the bridegroom. The groom may decide how many of the bridesmaids he would like to remain in the bed for the marriage consummation. However, if the bridegroom should dally with any of the bridesmaids in the middle of the night, the bride will proceed to thrash him with a slab of blubber or a moccasin.

A Japanese couple meet, chaperoned, for the first time before their marriage to see if they are satisfied with one another.

A Native wedding, Sefula, Central Africa.

It is an old Polish custom for the bride to send a surrogate to her wedding ceremony, usually a sister or close cousin disguised as the bride. The groom will do likewise, and send his best man, disguised as the real groom. The surrogate bride goes through the wedding ceremony and marriage consummation with the surrogate groom. If no evil befalls the surrogate couple within a fortnight, the real bride will agree to go through the wedding rites with the real groom.

♥

In Iran, it has been the custom that the groom not look, speak to, or touch his bride until the marriage is determined officially consummated.

A young couple are purified from all evil influences by pouring the blood of a sacrificed chicken over their heads; part of a ceremony among the Land Dyaks of the Sadong River in Sarawak.

The first German couple to marry on a loan supplied by the government: A gymnastics teacher of Aachen and his bride.

It is customary in Peru for the bridal party to decorate the honeymoon bed with red and green chile peppers to ensure a passionate and fruitful marriage.

♥

An old Scandinavian ritual demands that the bride perform the marriage ceremony with her shoes untied, and then walk to her honeymoon chamber wearing the same untied shoes. She proceeds to bed, consummates her marriage, and sleeps with the untied shoes dangling on her feet. It is the bride's hope that the shoes will fall off by themselves during the honeymoon-night activities, "so that she will bear children as easily as she removes her shoes."

♥

A Japanese wife must sleep with her head bowed to her husband and must not look him directly in the face during their marriage consummation, nor should her head be higher than his on the bed at any time on the honeymoon night. She must do this in deference to his male supremacy. If her husband should catch her sleeping with her head in a superior position to his, it is considered grounds for divorce.

A Polish wedding procession, Crakow, 1880.

In mountainous regions of Morocco, it is customary for the bridegroom to beat the bride between her shoulder blades with the cord of his dagger. This demonstrates his male supremacy. The bridegroom then inserts the dagger between the sheets of the honeymoon bed to ward off evil spirits during the marriage consummation. A similar wedding rite occurs in Croatia, except that the bridegroom boxes the bride's ears.

♥

An old Russian custom: The father of the bride leads his daughter to the bridegroom's bed. He then pulls out a new whip, and beats his daughter, declaring that he has whipped her for the last time. The father then hands the whip to the bridegroom, who demands that the bride pull off his boots. After the bride performs this task, the groom beats the bride on the head with his bootleg to ensure his authority. The bride then pours the groom a glass of vodka, which the groom proceeds to guzzle. It is then customary for the bride to wait for the groom's ceremonial belch, before he begins to consummate the marriage.

BIZARRE HONEYMOON RITES AMONG THE NACIREMA

Noted anthropologist Hubert T. Hordach spent fifteen years living among and studying the civilization of the Nacirema, a primitive tribe native to North America. This obscure tribe practices ceremonial rites that are similar to, and indicative of, the civilization of primitive man, six thousand years before the birth of Christ.

Hordach's prizewinning thesis, Life Among the Nacirema, has become a bible to all contemporary anthropologists involved in the studies of primitive civilizations. Hordach stated in his introduction that "the Nacirema society, though totally primitive, laid the foundations in behavioral psychology that can still be traced to today's American society. The Nacirema citizen was basically a being of minimal intelligence who was often industrious, jealous, suspicious, and warlike. They had the

peculiarity of being overly concerned with their bodily functions, and the evil spirit that they believed inhabited their bodies. They

Hubert T. Hordach

were highly dependent on their village witch doctor, who received their utmost deference. The Witch Doctor was usually the most revered and wealthy member of their community.

"However, despite their attention to their physical concerns, the Nacirema people tended to be sexually modest and re-

pressed. They were nearly always clothed, and were particularly concerned with correct tribal decoration."

Hordach made an in-depth study of Nacirema nuptial rituals in his chapter "The Nacirema Honeymoon." The following is an excerpt.

After the rather elaborate wedding rites, and the ceremonial feast, the young bride and groom disappeared from the other feasting tribesmen. I was told that they had left to discard their customary wedding robes, and decorate themselves for their ceremonial wedding night departure. This constituted the third change in body decoration for the bride and groom in one day. The fourth decoration process was yet to come.

At this point, young members of the wedding party began pushing toward us what appeared to be a strangely and elaborately decorated chariot. The chariot was covered with primitive paintings and what appeared to be hieroglyphics. Behind the chariot hung bright colored cloth, noise makers, and discarded sandals.

All at once, the bride and groom reappeared, freshly decorated. The festive villagers gathered about them and their families. The bride's face was painted in the ritualistic evening manner.

bride and groom surrounded the chariot of the newly-weds, in what became a sinister parade of noise-making, yelling and heckling. The racket continued until the procession was out of sight. Then, slowly, the young peers began to reappear at the village temple, but there was no sign of the bride and groom.

▌was soon informed that it was customary for the bride and groom to spend their wedding

Children properly attired for a Nacirema wedding.

but I was able to glean a few probable reasons for this. Because of the sexual taboos and the timidity of the Nacirema society, it was probably less embarrassing or stigmatizing for the young, newly-wed couple to perform their marital initiation away from their families and friends. Also, it was said that the newly-weds would have an easier time familiarizing themselves with the mysteries of one another without family interference.

The reason that seemed the most plausible to me however, was the fact that the newly-weds and/or their families had to pay a tribute in wampum to the neighboring village temple, for the newly-weds' post wedding visit. The inability to pay this tribute would cause shame and embarrassment to the families of the newly-weds, so the matter was deemed important and properly attended to.

Ritual headdress of a Nacirema groom.

Suddenly, the crowd began viciously pelting the bride and groom with some sort of grain, and they cruelly laughed and jeered at the newly-weds. The couple seemed to handle this situation with some embarrassment. However, the cruelty of the crowd apparently upset the bride's mother, who all at once began weeping.

Then a strange procession began. The young peers of the

night among strangers in a neighboring village. The natives of my village told me that all villages contained a special wedding night temple which they reserved for newly-weds of other villages. How long the newly-weds would stay at the foreign temple would often depend on the wealth and stature of their families.

No one seemed to have a distinct explanation as to why the newly-weds left their own village,

A popular Temple for Nacirema marriages.

I began interviewing many married women of my village to document what rites were included in the ritual wedding night ceremonies. They were all reluctant and ashamed to discuss this with me because any discussion of sexual activity is taboo and forbidden in the Nacirema society. But what they finally did tell me gave me a vague picture of the evening's activities.

When the wedding couple arrives at the marital temple, the husband is required to make a mark designating the couple officially as man and wife. (No couple is allowed to stay at the wedding night temple unless they are married.) They are then escorted into their marital chamber by one of the keepers of the temple, who is appropriately ceremonial, and accustomed to dealing with the embarrassment of newly-weds. The bridegroom pays homage to the keeper of the temple by presenting him with a small tribute of wampum (the richer the family, the bigger the tribute). At this point, the bridegroom examines the marital chamber to make sure that there

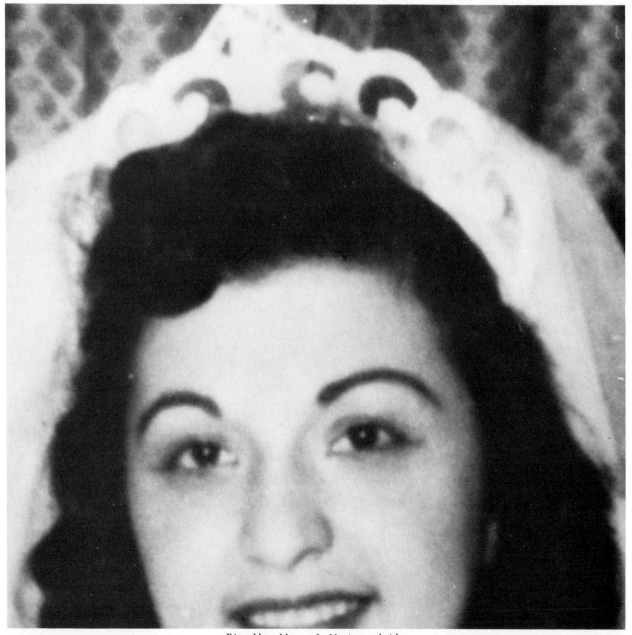

Ritual headdress of a Nacirema bride.

are no evil spirits lurking about. When the groom is satisfied that all is safe, he will suddenly lift his bride and hurtle her into the chamber.

The bride will compose herself and examine the chamber. If it meets with her satisfaction she will enter the sacred shrine. (All marital chambers contain a sacred shrine.) It is here that she pays homage to the Gods of the body. As the Nacirema believe that evil spirits come from human smells and excretions, the bride begins to mask these with sacred ointments that she has carried with her. She applies these ointments to all the potentially dangerous areas of her body, paying the greatest care to her mouth and genitalia. When she has finished with the body rites of the shrine, she dowses herself with holy water, and proceeds to change into her ritual wedding night robe. Then she begins to feel shy, and becomes afraid to leave the sanctity of the shrine. The amount of time spent in the shrine may vary from a few minutes, to hours, depending on the individual religious convictions of the bride. Some brides confessed to me that they knelt, wept, and prayed all night in the sacred shrine.

When the bride emerges from the shrine, the groom rises and proceeds to begin his own religious rites. The bride has now climbed into bed in his absence. She awaits the groom, nervously, in the dark.

A rare look at holy honeymoon shrines of the Nacirema.

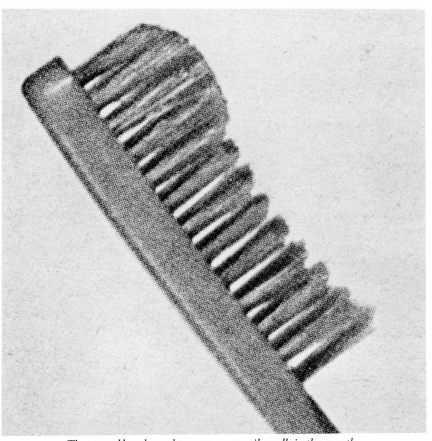

The sacred brush used to scare away evil smells in the mouth.

The groom will tend to perform his religious rites more quickly than the bride, as it appears within the Nacirema culture the women are more devoutly religious than the men. Nonetheless, the groom will take care not to subject his new wife to the dangerous evils of bodily smells. To insure his manliness, the bridegroom will often take a sharp knife and scrape his face in the area of his mouth and jaw. He does this carefully and lightly so that bleeding should not occur. He will also stand for a period of time, facing the shrine's altar to flex his muscles and pay homage to the God of masculinity. The bridegroom will then exhale loudly, and proceed to leave the shrine. He will have also changed into the sacred wedding night dress, and will eventually climb into bed beside his new wife.

The keeper of the village temple will have carefully left a bottle of sacramental mead on a small altar next to the wedding bed. The newly-weds will sip the sacrament before they begin their marital initiations.

I am told that the sacred marital initiation will take place at some time during the long dark night, but most Nacirema women were reluctant to discuss this rite. I also interviewed Nacirema husbands about the rite, but their answers were too wild and varying to be believed.

A Nacirema bride prepares for her ritual wedding night in the Temple.

•ALL ABOARD •
FOR THE WORLD'S FIRST SUPERSONIC
HONEYMOON

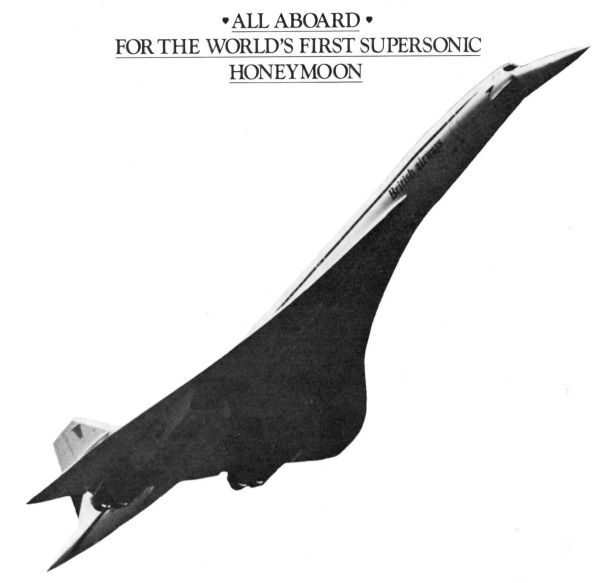

Phileas Fogg and Ali Khan, eat your hearts out. Here it is—the world's first supersonic honeymoon, an explorer's delight! Board your supersonic transport at Kennedy Airport, New York, U.S.A., and you proceed to take off and consummate your marriage over every continent in the world. Total flight time is estimated at sixteen hours and forty minutes.

Your marathon begins in New York City as you and your bride are plied with champagne and caviar in the glamorous first class lounge of Kennedy Airport.

You board your supersonic transport at 10:00 P.M. Our courteous flight attendants will lead you to your honeymoon cabin in the clouds. You will be ushered to a plush, suede-covered love seat, and belted down together for take-off. Once airborne, you may remove your seat belt and are free to wander around your cabin. At your disposal is a large refrigerator fully stocked with wines, delectable hors d'oeuvres, and a cold dinner platter. Behind your love seat you will find a comfortable king-size mattress, complete with silk sheets and two down pillows.

Remember, the object of your flight is to consummate your marriage over every continent in the world, so relax, and *pace yourself.* Here's an itinerary and checklist from your captain. Good luck!

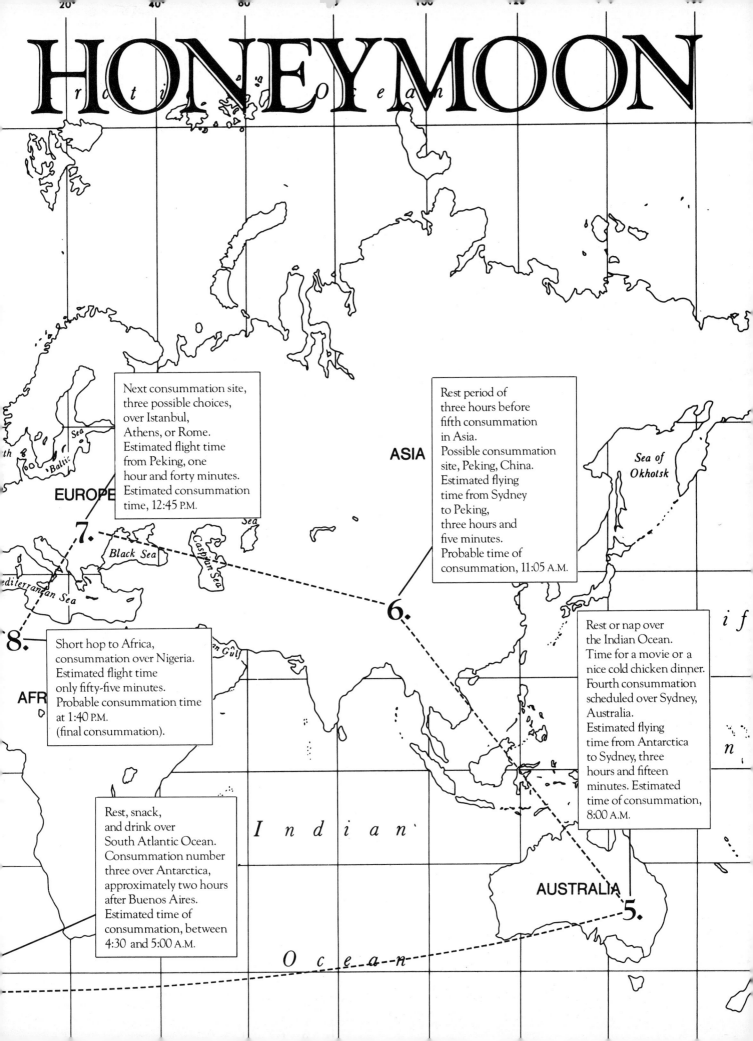

HONEYMOON

Next consumption site, three possible choices, over Istanbul, Athens, or Rome. Estimated flight time from Peking, one hour and forty minutes. Estimated consumption time, 12:45 P.M.

Rest period of three hours before fifth consummation in Asia. Possible consummation site, Peking, China. Estimated flying time from Sydney to Peking, three hours and five minutes. Probable time of consummation, 11:05 A.M.

Short hop to Africa, consummation over Nigeria. Estimated flight time only fifty-five minutes. Probable consummation time at 1:40 P.M. (final consummation).

Rest or nap over the Indian Ocean. Time for a movie or a nice cold chicken dinner. Fourth consummation scheduled over Sydney, Australia. Estimated flying time from Antarctica to Sydney, three hours and fifteen minutes. Estimated time of consummation, 8:00 A.M.

Rest, snack, and drink over South Atlantic Ocean. Consummation number three over Antarctica, approximately two hours after Buenos Aires. Estimated time of consummation, between 4:30 and 5:00 A.M.

EUROPE

ASIA

AFR

AUSTRALIA

7.

8.

6.

5.

• A HONEYMOON ON VENUS •

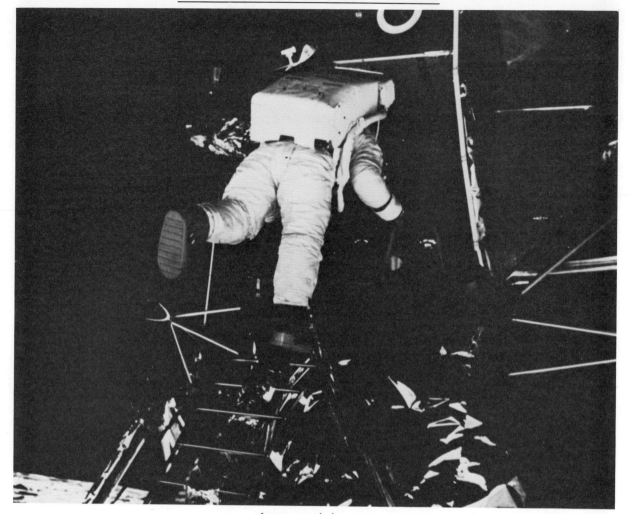

Love among the heavens.

It has to happen. The year is 2085. Mr. and Mrs. America are about to take off on the first interplanetary honeymoon to Venus. Now they are ushered into their own cushy heart-shaped rocket ship, appropriately named *Eros 1*. Countdown begins, and soon the newlyweds blast off to bliss, their honeymoon haven in the heavens.

The total flight time of *Eros 1* will be eighteen hours and twenty-four minutes. Seventeen minutes after takeoff, the rocket will jettison a stream of rubber shoes and cans into Earth's atmosphere where they will orbit Earth several times before disintegrating.

Mr. and Mrs. America will travel seventeen times faster than the speed of light. Just as they approach Venus, they will rendezvous with their appointed space station, *Honeymooner VII*. It is there that they will await the arrival of their own private honeymoon satellite, which will carry them on a seven-day orbit around Venus.

Mr. and Mrs. America will consummate their marriage in blessed privacy, all alone in outer space, and in a state of total weightlessness. Their honeymoon space satellite is a sphere made of fiberglass and designed for star gazing. They will glide gracefully above Venus's purple-blue cloud formations. There can be no more perfect way to begin a loving and beautiful marriage than to be circling the planet of love and beauty.

A Honeymoon Spacesuit

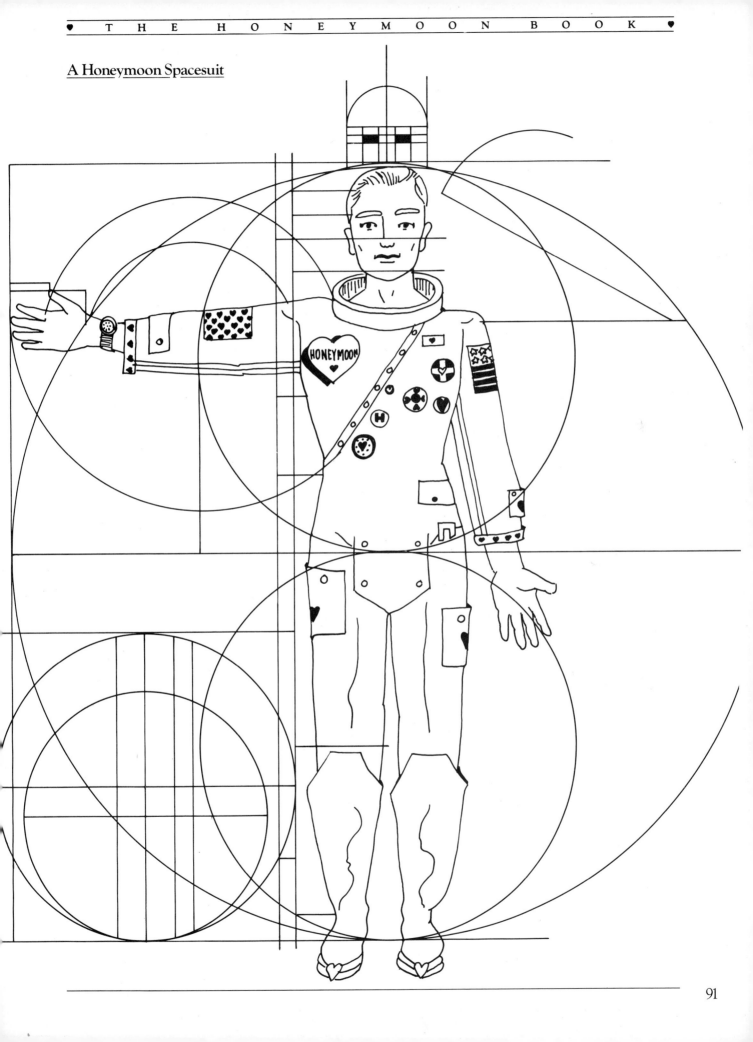

● Your Honeymoon Satellite ●

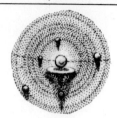

Before takeoff you will be issued your own personal spacesuit. Regulation honeymoon spacesuits are of a lean, streamlined design which handsomely exposes the form of the body. The suits are designed to unsnap easily and quickly, so at a critical moment, the 'mooners have easy access to one another. Spacesuits are made available in three different color combinations: bright yellow with navy blue piping, (the *Star Trek* look), white with blue piping and a red insignia (Jordache for NASA), or the first totally flesh-colored suit (designed by the engineers at Johnson & Johnson). All suits come equipped with matching helmets, gloves, and oxygen packs. The suits are heat and water resistant as well as anti-radioactive.

The interior of the glass honeymoon satellite is divided into three living compartments. The largest area is the gaming, or "play," quarters, where the honeymooners may view Venus and enjoy a totally weightless paradise. The play quarters are furnished with continually floating soft vinyl furniture, all of which is equipped with seat belts. If the 'mooners should get tired of floating around, they can easily belt themselves down on one of the cushy floating couches. The play quarters are also stocked with a large variety of games, such as an inflatable plastic Ping-Pong table, a magnetic dartboard complete with Styrofoam darts, and a leather card table with an adherent tabletop, magnetic Scrabble, magnetic chess, and magnetic backgammon.

The second largest area in the honeymoon satellite is the control room and dining area, where a state of simulated gravity exists. This room contains all the necessary radio and monitor equipment needed to keep the honeymoon satellite healthily in orbit, and to avoid collision with random meteors and asteroids. It is enjoyable to watch the controls, but one need never operate them, because the satellite is actually run by a computer which is monitored at the space station *Honeymooner VII*. The control room is also equipped with a wide-screen movie theater. In addition the control room houses a fabulous kitchen where the meals of one's heart's desire are at push-button convenience.

The sleeping quarters exist as a semi-weightless room. The large comfortable honeymoon bed is bolted to the floor, as are the night table and clock radio. The honeymoon couple, however, is free to float about, or they have the option of strapping themselves to the bed with NASA's specially designed magnetic rubber sheets. If the couple plans to spend their sleeping hours floating about the room, all is safe because the room is "snooze proof." There are no sharp corners for floating sleepers to contend with, and the walls are padded.

The honeymoon lavatory, which adjoins the sleeping chamber, is totally magnetized, and it is advisable for all honeymooners to wear special magnetized slippers, issued by NASA, when using this chamber. It should also be noted that certain ordinary health rituals, such as applying toothpaste to a toothbrush, will be conducted with some difficulty, and so a NASA training program is mandatory for all honeymooning space cadets.

Love among the heavens.

• How to Pack for a Weightless Honeymoon •

Your spacesuits are provided for you and so is your food. The satellite accommodations are superb. But in order to keep a little "earthliness" in your honeymoon, here is a checklist of what you might want to bring along from your home planet.

WOMEN

LINGERIE AND NIGHTWEAR. Make sure it's cotton, because silk and polyester stick to the rubber sheets.

BATHROBES. Buy something fitting or else you may get tangled up in your clothing during a free fall.

SLACKS. You may get bored in your spacesuits, so elastic ski pants are the most practical for all areas of the satellite; running pants and sweatsuits are also a good idea. Avoid bell-bottoms at all costs.

SHIRTS, BLOUSES, AND SWEATERS. Avoid anything very flouncy. T-shirts are a good idea, so are Danskins. Most sweaters are comfortable and safe, but turtlenecks can be a little constraining.

SKIRTS. Pack one skirt for that "special night." Your husband will love it when you float around the gaming room. Your best bets are A-lines or pleated ones (dirndl style also works well). *Avoid bell-bottoms at all costs.*

SHOES. Oxfords and sneakers are a good idea. They may be unflattering, but high heels are very dangerous in a free fall. Pumps will fall off. Any thing low-heeled with a strap or tie is a good bet.

COSMETICS. Avoid anything bottled. Shampoo, facial cream, perfumes, and toothpaste should all be contained in tubes. All aerosol sprays are a total waste of time, and can be messy and dangerous. A note on makeup: It would be helpful if you could have any metallic-cased makeup such as lipstick, eye pencil, and mascara magnetized for your storing convenience.

MEN

UNDERWEAR. Make it brief! Boxer shorts will be too bulky!

PAJAMAS. Cotton only. *No polyester.* Your best bet for sleeping is an undershirt and pajama bottoms, or better still, nothing at all!

SHIRTS. Avoid anything starched. Lacoste golf shirts are a good idea. Best bet: Jersey polo shirts of any variety.

TROUSERS. Keep them casual. Straight slacks and worn-in blue jeans are a good idea. Avoid stiff jeans at all costs.

JACKETS AND TIES. You don't need them. Jackets are cumbersome and ties are dangerous.

SHOES. Sorry, no loafers. Tennis or running shoes are the most reliable. A pair of wing-tipped oxfords can add a nice dressy touch.

TOILETRIES. Hand razors are dangerous here, even if magnetized. Electric razors are much safer. If you carry any sharp instrument such as manicure scissors, make sure it can be securely fastened in a safe place when you are not using it. Avoid bottle cosmetics and carry only tubed liquids. Please, *no spray deodorants.*

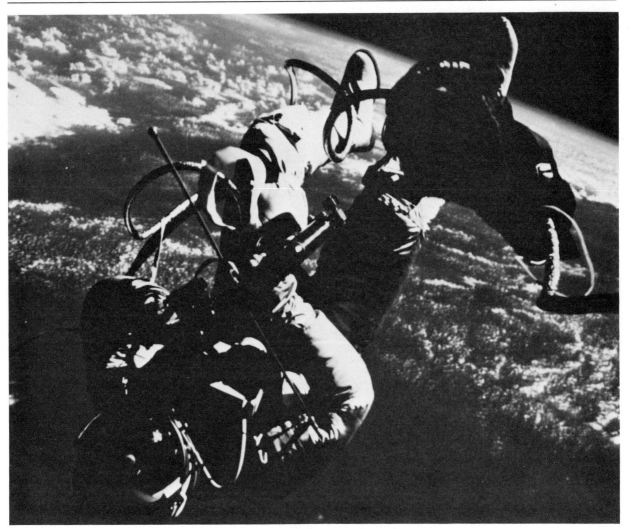

● COMING SOON! ●
MORE PLANETARY RESORTS!

Because of its mythical association with love and beauty and its prox-
imity to the planet Earth, Venus is the obvious first choice for a honeymoon
haven in outer space. But when the rest of the world catches up with NASA,
Venus will become a very crowded resort and much less romantic.

In our continuing search for new frontiers, the scientists of NASA
who gave you a honeymoon on Venus will soon give you other planetary resorts that will certainly be as desirable, and as accessible as your own backyard.

Mercury will soon be featured as an ideal place for all us sun worship-
ers. Our new Caribbean in the heavens will feature satellites that come complete with their own swimming pool and sauna.

Attention outdoorsmen and camera buffs! Scientists are now complet-
ing the Honeymoon on Mars project. Trips to Mars will include floating tours
of the planet. This exciting honeymoon will be more adventuresome and rigorous than a raft ride on the Colorado rapids!

For those of us who are naturally cosmopolitan, Jupiter will be the
proverbial Big Apple of outer space. Massive shopping centers (all duty free)
will be constructed in huge floating space stations. There will also be an abundance of floating restaurants, theaters, and art galleries. This is definitely a honeymoon for the culturally minded, and it is no longer a light year away!

CHAPTER FIVE

POSTCARDS FROM AMERICA HONEYMOON U.S.A.

When we think of honeymoons in America, Niagara Falls, Atlantic City, and the Poconos immediately come to mind as those places most often chosen as a honeymoon spot. Each in its turn has been the most popular honeymoon haven in the United States. Their popularity has been matched only by Las Vegas and Miami Beach, the most popular spots of today.

None of these cities would be considered a glamour capital of the world (though Las Vegas certainly has its own special appeal), but in their various heydays, each place has held the mystical key to romance for honeymooners.

The following is a nostalgic look at America's favorite honeymoon playgrounds.

· Niagara Falls ·

*Now that we have had the rice and flowers
the knot is tied;
I can visualize such happy hours,
close by your side.
The honeymoon in store is one that you'll adore,
I'm gonna take you for a ride.
I'll go home and get my panties, you go home and get your scanties,
And away we'll go. Mm!——
Off we're gonna shuffle, shuffle off to Buffalo.
To Niagara in a sleeper, there's no honeymoon that's cheaper,
And the train goes slow. Ohh!——
Off we're gonna shuffle, shuffle off to Buffalo.
Someday, the stork may pay a visit, and leave a little souvenir.
Just a little cute "what is it," but we'll discuss that later dear.
For a little silver quarter, we can have the pullman porter
Turn the lights down low. Ooh!——
Off we're gonna shuffle, shuffle off to Buffalo.
Shuffle off to Buffalo.*

"Shuffle Off to Buffalo."
Music by Harry Warren, Lyrics by Al Dubin, from the
Warner Brothers musical *42nd Street*

SOUVENIR FOLDER of NIAGARA FALLS

POSTAGE 1½c WITHOUT MESSAGE

General View of Niagara Falls

Niagara Falls, New York, may be the most famous honeymoon watering hole in the U.S.A. It certainly has the qualities of everyone's ideal romantic haven for newlyweds. In the past, it was popular for couples to be married quickly in Buffalo, New York, and then hop a bus to spend a blissful wedding night in a cozy love nest near the falls.

The initial appeal of Niagara Falls to honeymooners is obvious. Waterfalls are romantic to begin with, and Niagara Falls are the biggest waterfalls in the United States. Niagara Falls, New York, also borders on Canada, so it picks up some of the romance of a border town. It's a little bit like making love at the end of the world.

It may be that Niagara Falls and romance became synonymous because the power, force, and beauty of the falls remind us, in some ways, of the human orgasm, much the way fireworks and trains roaring through tunnels are used metaphorically in movies. Watching the falls is sexy and inspirational. There are few things more romantic than a stroll on the Honeymoon Trail near the falls. That romantic hike usually culminates in intense spooning. When the sun sets, the honeymooners can return to their love nest and practice what was inspired by their view of the falls.

The fact of the matter is that Niagara Falls is not a terrific place to be unless you happen to be on a honeymoon. With the exception of a magnificent view of a magnificent piece of nature's handiwork, there isn't very much going on there that cannot be had, better, somewhere else in the United States. But honeymooners are content to look at the falls, sigh, and make love, which is, of course, what honeymoons are all about.

Though the spot has in recent times lost some of its appeal as a honeymoon resort, the ideal of Niagara's romance lives on forever, and some loving innocents among us continue to "Shuffle Off to Buffalo."

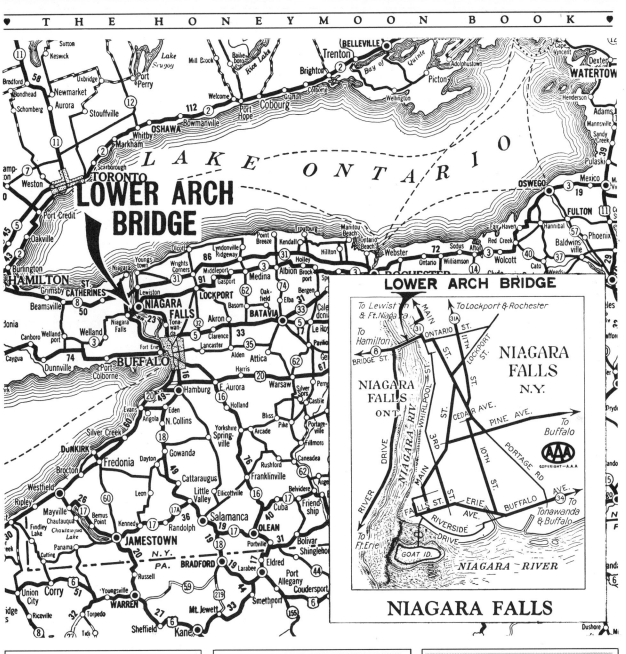

LOWER ARCH BRIDGE

NIAGARA FALLS

NIAGARA FALLS, N.Y.

274:—Rock of Ages and Cave of the Winds, Niagara Falls.

276—THE LEGEND OF THE WHITE CANOE, NIAGARA FALLS.

451—AMERICAN FALLS FROM BELOW, NIAGARA FALLS.

99

·Atlantic City·

It is a city built on sand, and it happens to be where it is because that is the closest place to Philadelphia that is on the sea. By the end of the nineteenth century, Atlantic City had become "the Queen of Resorts." It was also Honeymoon Capital, U.S.A.

The attraction of Atlantic City as a honeymoon resort is also clearly apparent. There are the sun and the sea. There is a boardwalk. By 1896 a boardwalk four miles long and forty feet wide had been built as a huge promenade for the sunbathers. The boardwalk was lined with fabulous stores and entertainment attractions. What could be more fun or romantic for young lovers? By the early nineteen hundreds the boardwalk had earned a reputation. It was sexy.

Atlantic City offered its newlywed visitors a plethora of fabulous hotels and honeymoon cottages to choose from. The city was so proud to be host to newlyweds that it formed its own Honeymoon Club. The certificate of the club states—

This is to certify that _____ did celebrate their entry into the sea of matrimony by honeymooning in Atlantic City, New Jersey, Honeymoon Capital of the nation. All of those certain rights and privileges which are accorded to honeymooners in Atlantic City are hereby granted them, with all our best wishes for many years of wedded happiness.

Signed The mayor of Atlantic City

Though toward the middle of the twentieth century Atlantic City's romance, glamour, and charm began to fade, the recent legalization of casino gambling may lead to its once again becoming the Queen of Resorts.

Steeplechase Pier, Atlantic City, N.J.

GREEN'S, DUNLOP AND CHALFONTE HOTELS,
BOARD WALK,
ATLANTIC CITY, N.J.

· Miami Beach ·

In the midthirties, Miami Beach began to compete with Atlantic City as a seaside honeymoon capital. By the late nineteen fifties, it had surpassed the Queen of Resorts. Of course, Miami Beach had an edge over Atlantic City. It was warm all year long and provided a haven for December brides.

The array of glamorous hotels on Collins Avenue expanded every year, and every year more and more honeymooners arrived to get their feet wet. As the honeymooners and tourists arrived, so did famous entertainers, who performed in various hotels and created Miami Beach's nightlife. There was also the attraction of nearby Hialeah racetrack, where the honeymooners could gamble away some of their wedding money. A visit to Flamingo Grove also served to enhance romance.

A honeymoon in Miami Beach was designed to be fun, and it was. Who knows if having so much fun on the honeymoon makes for trouble when it's time to settle into "real life"?

PAN-AMERICAN TERMINAL, MIAMI, FLA.

View from Bayfront Park, Miami, Florida

SHOWING "McALLISTER", "COLUMBUS" and "MIAMI COLONIAL" HOTELS

Horses Parading before a Race, Hialeah Park, Miami

· Las Vegas ·

It always made sense to go to Las Vegas to get married because of Nevada's liberal and uncomplicated marriage laws. Perhaps it made even greater sense to go to Las Vegas to get a divorce. But, as Vegas honeymooners know, Reno has become the divorce capital, and Vegas is *the* place to come to have a good time.

As a honeymoon haven, Las Vegas started out with legal gambling plus an array of motor courts in which the wedding night could be gloriously passed. Some of the motor courts even had a swimming pool.

In the nineteen thirties, Las Vegas was still a rinky-dink town of questionable morals. By the nineteen fifties it was the pleasure palace of the United States. Glamorous hotels, glamorous gambling casinos, and glamorous swimming pools were followed by even more glamorous entertainment. Nightclub acts in Vegas became the greatest spectacles in the world, even rivaling the gambling casinos as the town's primary attraction.

The major industry of Las Vegas is pleasure. The desert climate is beautiful. A honeymoon day in Las Vegas would include a late and luxurious breakfast, a midday swim, a nap before dinner, evening show, and all-night gambling. Honeymoons in Vegas are fun. The problem, often, is that they are over too quickly.

· The Poconos ·

The brochure copy for COVE HAVEN, a honeymoon resort in the heart of the beautiful Poconos reads as follows:

The moment the two of you step into your Garden of Eden Apple…you will be the only couple in the world. Each couple can discover a total world of privacy. Cozy up in front of a log-burning fireplace. Dive into devilish delights in your very own indoor private swimming pool, completely surrounded by mirrored walls that reflect your every fantasy. From the pool, step into your own sauna or pass through arched doors that lead into the most magnificent of bedrooms…it is here where you can share life's beginning…love's never ending. A place that assures you total privacy from the rest of the world—complete with the unique, twin-sized, sunken, heart-shaped "sweetheart" bath, color TV, carpeted floors and walls, personal refrigerator, curved steps and mirrored headboard…all to make your honeymoon a total experience.

—from a promotional brochure for
Cove Haven in the Poconos

Poconos

Cove Haven, in Lakeville, Pennsylvania, and many other resorts in the Poconos just like it attempt to create the perfect fantasy honeymoon for American couples. Where else but in the Poconos can one find heart-shaped tubs, beds, and pools? Where else can one be assured that ceilings and walls will be mirrored for double honeymoon excitement?

Year after year, honeymooners arrive at the Poconos by the thousands to ensure themselves the perfect honeymoon. What Niagara Falls provides in lyrical romance, the resorts of the Poconos provide in curriculum.

The Pocono mountains are beautiful, and the honeymooners can take walks or go skiing or swimming, but then again, they can do that almost anywhere. A luxurious bubble bath in a heart-shaped tub is a sexy experience that happens once in a lifetime. (Honeymoons are *meant* to happen once in a lifetime, although we all know the truth about that.)

What mainly draws couples to these thriving gardens of Eden is that the Poconos resorts promise to cater to the honeymooner's every need, even if the honeymooners aren't sure what their needs are.

Oh,
how you'll
love to get up
in the morning
to breakfast in bed
at the Summit.

There's no end to the rainbow of outdoor and indoor pleasures. Summer, Winter, Spring and Fall, the Summit is a Pocono playground of sensational outdoor sports and activities. Indoors our fabulous new Sports Spectrum offers you tennis, ice skating and sports galore. The flashing lights, buzzers and bells of the Arcade is music to the ears of billiard buffs, pinball wizards, ping-pong players and spectators alike. Set out treasure hunting for gifts you'll always remember in the fascinating Bazaar Shop, and to top it off there are mountainous, mouth watering Sundaes and many other delicious treats to satisfy the urge at our Snack Bar.

The once in a lifetime Summit Honeymoon promises you a lifetime of joyous memories of the new found happiness you'll both share here together.

POCONO PALACE

Club Lodge Room

Deluxe accommodation, offering a Panoramic View of beautiful Echo Lake, king size round bed with mirrored headboard, and standard bath with shower. Popular accommodation convenient to all of Pocono Palace's wide array of facilities. Individually controlled heat and air conditioning, color T.V. and telephone.

Welcome to the Wonderful World of Caesar's Honeymoon Resorts

The Poconos are honeymoon country, no doubt about it! There are many resorts ... you can choose only one for your honeymoon. It must be the right one! Your honeymoon must be all that you've dreamed of since you realized that someday you would have a love of your own. That's why ...

COVE HAVEN, PARADISE STREAM AND POCONO PALACE. Enclosed you will find descriptive brochures on the three leading honeymoon resorts in the Pocono Mountains of Pennsylvania. Cove Haven, for many years and still the most desired of all honeymoon resorts, now has two companion resorts; Paradise Stream, uniquely charming with a quiet grace; and Pocono Palace, new and excitingly sports-oriented, allow you to choose the honeymoon haven of your dreams.

Our low cost, all-inclusive Package Plans feature free-of-charge all activities, meals and entertainment. Regardless of which resort you choose, you are welcome to use the facilities at all three, making our resorts your best choice for a fun-filled and memorable honeymoon.

You are invited first-hand to come and visit with us, and to let us show you around in order to view for yourselves the many varied and beautiful facilities and accommodations awaiting you. We sincerely look forward to being your host for this Once-In-A-Lifetime occasion. Let us help to make your honeymoon a most special time ... Together.

With Love,

Adam and Eve

Adam & Eve

HONEYMOON HOTEL

WARNER BROS. PRESENT

FOOTLIGHT PARADE

WORDS BY
AL DUBIN
MUSIC BY
HARRY WARREN

DIRECTED BY
LLOYD BACON AND
BUSBY BERKELEY•

JAMES CAGNEY

JOAN BLONDELL

RUBY KEELER

DICK POWELL

M. WITMARK & SONS
NEW YORK
B. FELDMAN & CO., LONDON, ENG.
MADE IN U.S.A.

CHAPTER SIX

HOLLYWOOD HONEYMOONS

How am I to say
What I want to say
In the proper way, my dear?
I'm not a gallant cavalier,
But I'm sincere

So I'm gonna say
All I have to say,
In the language of the day.
You may have heard it all before
But here it goes once more—

How about a little celebration
To the jingle of the wedding bell?
How about a little reservation
At the Honeymoon Hotel?

Honeymooning's gonna be my hobby,
Don't you think a honeymoon is swell?
Wait until we walk into the lobby
Of the Honeymoon Hotel.

Cupid is the night clerk
'Neath the stars above,
He just loves his night work
And we just love to love.

Oh, I'm a mister looking for a missus,
As a missus you'll do very well,
Bring along your things and all your kisses
To the Honeymoon Hotel.

Words to the song "Honeymoon Hotel," lyrics by Al Dubin, music by Harry Warren. From *Footlight Parade*, directed by Busby Berkeley, 1934.

♥   ♥   ♥

Let's face it. Life is a movie. Sometimes even a big splashy musical like the ones Busby Berkeley used to make. Whatever experiences grant us our perceptions of male-female relationships, never are they more strongly reinforced—and manipulated—than through the movies. We have fashioned our lives and our romantic ideals (not to mention our morality) by the ever-changing role models sent our way by Hollywood and television.

Doris Day

In the late fifties and early sixties, we knew that Doris Day had never made love without legal marriage and a honeymoon. (At the same time we realized that Marilyn Monroe was making whoopee all over the place, but considering her physiology, one had to make exceptions. Of course we could aspire to be Marilyn Monroe, as a great many of us aspire to be Mozart or Picasso, but the more realistic of us set our sights lower and aspired to be cute and perky like Doris Day.)

In a series of how-do-you-tell-them-apart movies we found our poor Doris *almost* compromised by all sorts of beastly, panting, lusting, indecent men. (The male leads were generally dark and hairy, making our plucky blonde heroine seem all the more vulnerable.)

Doris Day and Rock Hudson in "Lover Come Back"

In *Lover Come Back*, we encounter Doris as a successful advertising executive who is warring with a despicable and unscrupulous Rock Hudson. Hudson runs a rival ad agency. We watch the devilish Hudson pull all sorts of shenanigans and charades to lure Doris into bed, while he simultaneously is trying to steal away her advertising accounts.

At one point, Doris almost succumbs to an elaborate Hudson ruse. To heighten the dramatic effect of her imminent plunge, she wistfully sings "Should I Surrender?" Fortunately she discovers just in time that Hudson is a cad. Flying into a rage, she throws him out of her apartment.

Hudson does finally succeed in compromising Doris, but only when they are both under the influence of a new product called "Vip." Vip is a miracle drug that has the potency of five martinis. To our shock and dismay, we discover the two waking up together in a seedy motel in Maryland. Just when we have begun to lose all respect for Doris we find to our relief (but not surprise) that they had been married first and that we are witnessing the aftermath of their wedding night.

Their marriage has made everything kosher, but for Ms. Day there will be no honeymoon without the presence of true love. So we applaud her as she storms out on Rock Hudson and has her marriage annulled. Of course, nine months later, poor Doris pays the consequences of her wedding night in the sack, and we see her rushing to the maternity ward. Yet we know that Rock Hudson has always truly loved her, no matter how big a cad he might have been. They remarry minutes before she goes into heavy labor and have their honeymoon in the delivery room.

In Doris Day movies, her sexual standards extended to every other character as well. James Garner, who played Doris's husband in *Move Over Darling*, inadvertently married Polly Bergen because he believed that Doris was dead. (Doris had been missing for five years after her plane crashed at sea, and the court ruled her officially dead even though there has been no trace of her body.)

James Garner, Polly Bergen (right) and Thelma Ritter in "Move Over Darling"

On Garner's wedding night with Polly Bergen, Doris miraculously turns up just in time to prevent the unknowing Garner from committing sinful adultery. Garner is then put in the awkward position of telling Polly Bergen that his first wife is still alive and that the honeymoon is over before it has even begun. Doris, in the meantime, is furious at the fact that Garner has taken Bergen to the same hotel for a honeymoon that he had taken *her* for *their* honeymoon. Garner argues that it had always been a very nice, well-run hotel. And throughout the whole to do, poor, frustrated, doubly married Garner can't sleep with either wife in the "nice" hotel until he straightens the mess out.

While figuring out some way to break the news to Bergen, Garner makes her believe that he is impotent, a task that Bergen makes even more difficult by being a most seductive honeymooner.

Garner has some revenge on Doris when he finds out that for the past five years she has been living on a tropical island with brawny Chuck Connors, another survivor of the plane wreck. Garner conjures up images of Doris and Connors, lying in the sun scantily clad, taking bites from the same apple. Garner angrily accuses Doris of being unfaithful to him. We all know it isn't true. Handsome, virile Connors may have unsuccessfully chased a reluctant Doris around the tropical island for five years, but Doris would never succumb to his lewd advances. No wedding—no sex.

(*Move Over Darling* was a remake of the mid-thirties movie *My Favorite Wife*, starring Cary Grant and Irene Dunne. The story line is basically the same, except that it is possible that Irene Dunne *had* dallied on that tropical island. The movie was originally going to be remade as *Something's Got to Give*, featuring Marilyn Monroe and Dean Martin. That would have been a very different picture altogether.)

The sexual mores of early-sixties Doris Day movies were a giant step backward in the sexual enlightenment of the film industry. (A favorite comment of Hollywood producers on the subject of Doris Day was, "I knew her before she was a virgin.") In the twenties, silent films contained a much looser morality. Actors and actresses appeared to be making mad, passionate, sinful love all over the place. And it wasn't long until the personal morality of those within the Hollywood industry fell into public question when sex scandals of the stars were reported with relish in the newspapers.

Cary Grant and Irene Dunne in "My Favorite Wife"

Effects of The Hays Commission

What happened was that Hollywood censored itself before the public could, formed the Hays Commission, and our cinematic sex lives were cleaned up considerably. Now it was forbidden for movies to imply that any sexual intercourse had taken place before a wedding. There were noted exceptions to this, but the story line of the excepted movie had to make a strong moral point emphasizing the dangers of premarital relationships.

Irene Rich in "My Official Wife"

In 1926, for instance, Warner Brothers released a movie called *My Official Wife*, in which Irene Rich played a nobleman's daughter who was dressed up as a peasant to attend a fancy-dress ball. On her way to the ball, she is abducted by six men, one of whom rapes her. She seeks revenge on the rapist, but then falls in love with him instead. When she marries her rapist, all is set right, making even rape a prelude to honeymoons.

Cheaper to Marry, an MGM production of 1924, was a Hays Commission favorite because the movie preached that matrimony was not only a "good thing," but created a great financial deal for its partners as well.

The idea of divorce also, was basically taboo in the movie industry. In order to obtain a movie divorce, one of the cinematic partners had to be so overtly disgusting that the audience would believe that in this special instance, divorce was a matter of life and death.

The Honeymoon Express portrays a marriage where the husband's boozing, his inability to provide for his family, and his sinful infidelities were so heinous, they seriously threatened the lives and well-being of his wife and children. The wife rightfully dumps him (fortunately she has remained tremendously attractive, despite the horrors of her marriage) and is free to go about seeking a suitable husband and father for her children. Her new amorous adventures are designed to amuse us, but we never lose sight of the fact that this woman needs to find herself a husband (as the movie's title illustrates) and is not out to just mess around.

Buster Keaton and Dorothy Sebastian in "Spite Marriage"

There weren't many movies made about honeymoons, because film-makers were not allowed to film what generally goes on during them. There-fore, only comical, problematic honeymoons could be filmed. One of these, *Honeymoon—1928*, was a story about a honeymoon that turns into a fiasco be-cause a rival of the groom has sent a dog along as a wedding present. The dog has been carefully trained to let nobody, but nobody, touch the bride. In the end the honeymoon is saved when the dog falls in love with a fluffy white cat.

In *Spite Marriage*, Buster Keaton and Dorothy Sebastian make honey-moon history. Dorothy drinks and carries on during their wedding festivities only to pass out later on the marriage bed. What follows is a memorable bit of comedy genius, as Keaton attempts to spend an amorous honeymoon with his now far-gone wife.

The fact of the matter is that infidelity, adultery, and torrid sex made for much more interesting movie-going than the legal, sin-free sex of happily mar-ried couples. So the Hollywood movie moguls designed a series of plots cen-tered around whether or not the couple's marriage was legal. These movies could pass the strict codes of the Hays Commission and, at the same time, appear to contain a little pre nuptial sex, a little lust, and just a touch of adultery.

Robert Young (center) in "Bridal Suite"

In *The Love Racket* (1929) a husband tells his unsuspecting wife—after their wedding night—that they are not legally married. He then proceeds to walk out on her, making this the world's most complicated one-night stand. Years later, the jilted wife finds herself sitting on a jury where a young woman is being tried for murdering a man who married her, made love to her (on their supposed wedding night), and then, after claiming that the marriage wasn't legal, abandoned her. The man, of course, turns out to be the heroine's ex-husband, making this movie more appropriately titled *Love 'Em and Leave 'Em*.

In *Bridal Suite*, playboy Robert Young woos them, promises to wed them, and leaves them standing at the altar. (This brings to mind a title like "Almost Love 'Em and Leave 'Em.") In this film, however, Young finally gets caught at the altar and subsequently rights all wrongs.

In *Public Wedding* (1936), Jane Wyman and William Hopper play a couple of down-on-their-luck itinerant show people. To attract an audience to their traveling sideshow, they stage a fake public wedding in the mouth of a stuffed whale. Predictably, they find out that in the process they have actually been legally married, so after handling a few minor complications, they decide to go on a honeymoon and fall in love.

Jane Wyman, William Hopper in "Public Wedding"   Ann Sheridan in "The Footloose Heiress"

Marrying for Money

Ann Sheridan honeymoons on a bet in *The Footloose Heiress*. She elopes with poor, but honorable, Craig Reynolds. The wager had been one that would have her married by midnight of her eighteenth birthday, and the reward was five thousand dollars. She succeeds in winning the money, and what turns out to be the perfect mate as well.

In *Mr. Skeffington*, Bette Davis marries millionaire Claude Rains in order to wipe out her irresponsible brother's enormous debt to him. They honeymoon aboard the Staten Island Ferry (a rather penurious gesture, for all Skeffington's millions), watching other honeymooning couples who are genuinely in love. Though Rains has known all along that Davis doesn't love him and married him for his money, it takes two more reels of film for us to watch Davis have a baby that she doesn't really want, retain her old suitors, to Skeffington's dismay, divorce Skeffington for an enormous settlement, come down with diphtheria, lose her fabulous beauty, not to mention her hair, and witness Claude Rains' loss of eyesight from the atrocities inflicted on him by Nazis, before she realizes that she did indeed love the man she married.

Claude Rains, (lower left) and Bette Davis in "Mr. Skeffington"

Several inheritance movies work out well for potential celluloid honeymooners. Joan Leslie finds that she can inherit ten million dollars if she marries a man of superior intelligence on a certain date (*Cinderella Jones*, 1946). She finds and marries her intellectual, who just happens to be the dashing Robert Alda, and has a honeymoon of love, money, and mental enlightenment.

In *Brewster's Millions*, Dennis O'Keefe has to spend a million dollars in a given period of time and leave himself without an asset to his name, in order to inherit another ten million dollars. The complicated will of a long-lost uncle stipulates that he also tell no one about this until the million dollars has properly vanished. While going about the task, O'Keefe keeps his fiancée virtually waiting at the altar through the entire picture. Every time he spends money he ends up making more. Finally, he rids himself of all the money just in time to wed his bride, who was about to jilt him. He gets his girl and his ten million.

Sex and the Married Girl

Katharine Hepburn and Spencer Tracy introduce us to a sexless marriage in *Without Love*. Tracy plays an aerospace engineer who is fed up with the shenanigans of women, and is interested only in his work. After World War II he comes to Washington, D.C., to work on a top-secret project. There is a housing shortage at the time, and Katharine Hepburn offers to let him carry out his important experiment in her basement. She even volunteers to be his assistant. She then proposes a marriage of convenience without love, and Tracy, who has no patience for the frivolities of romance, agrees. They spend their honeymoon working in the basement laboratory. But, alas, love blooms in the basement, and they end up sparring and making each other jealous, until they realize that their loveless marriage isn't loveless after all.

Katharine Hepburn and Spencer Tracy in "Without Love"

Perhaps the archetypal movie reflecting Hollywood's attitudes toward marriage and sex is *It Happened One Night*. Claudette Colbert plays a wealthy heiress on the lam from an intended spouse and a dominating father, who is insisting that she marry the creep. She is discovered by a cynical, somewhat socialistic newspaper reporter (Clark Gable, no less), who learns that Colbert had not been kidnapped, as her father believes. He wants her exclusive story, and convinces her to travel around with him for protection. When, posing as young marrieds, they share a motel room, Gable chivalrously hangs a blanket between their twin beds, which he dubs "The Walls of Jericho." After they endure all sorts of craziness together they realize that they are in love. Lo and behold, it turns out that Colbert's oppressive father actually approves of uncouth Gable. The movie ends with a Gable-Colbert wedding night, and as Gable blows a trumpet, "The Walls of Jericho" come tumbling down.

Claudette Colbert and Clark Gable in "It Happened One Night"

Bette Davis, Gene Raymond in "Ex-Lady"

The virtues of marriage, and the dangers of preconnubial living arrangements, were illustrated in a relatively liberated movie called *Ex-Lady*. An advertising writer (Gene Raymond) is in love with a commercial artist (Bette Davis). She has the advanced idea that living together outside the protective legality of marriage is an arrangement superior to conventional marriage. She believes that the emancipated woman should have complete independence in love, and that marriage kills romance. In the beginning he gives her a chance to try out her ideas. All works out well with their living arrangement until Raymond starts his own agency. Arguing that a life of sin won't win him any clients, he urges Davis to marry him. She reluctantly gives in, but is afraid that their marriage will only destroy their relationship. Raymond makes her head of his art department so that she can be around to keep an eye on him.

Their business becomes successful, and they even make enough money to take a fancy honeymoon trip to Havana. When they come back from Havana, though, they find, to their dismay, that they have lost a lot of important clients. Each blames the other for this setback.

While rebuilding the business, Raymond pays a lot of undue attention to a beautiful, wealthy client. Davis begins to believe that he is having an affair with her. They argue, and Raymond moves out of their apartment. Then Davis tries to woo Raymond back to their premarital status. Raymond likes this idea because, he claims, he is enjoying his freedom. Davis is furious with this and puts herself in a compromising situation with another man to make Raymond jealous. It works. Suddenly, they patch everything up and decide to remain married. Why they do is a complete mystery, but Hollywood would never imply that marriage and honeymoons could in any way destroy a person's or a couple's happiness.

True Love?

Accidental marriages and honeymoons were terrific for Hollywood because the couple could have sex and fall in love later, and the Hays Commission was as happy as the audiences.

In *The Girl from Tenth Avenue* (1935) Ian Hunter goes out on a drunk after he is ditched by his bitchy fiancée. He wakes up the next morning married to a girl he has never met before who, of course, adores him, and also happens to be Bette Davis. Naturally, the nasty fiancée wants him back, but he soon realizes that he is in love with the girl he accidentally married, who also happens to be beneath his station. This movie made honeymooning on a drunk an ideal situation.

Bette Davis, Ian Hunter in "The Girl From Tenth Avenue"

Cary Grant and Eva Marie Saint in "North by Northwest"

Alfred Hitchcock often liked his hair-raising movies to end with a happily-ever-after honeymoon. The fact that the beleaguered couple had to endure all kinds of monstrosities beforehand has probably made Hitchcock the kinkiest of love-story makers. In *North by Northwest*, we watch Cary Grant perform death-defying feats of immense bravery and intelligence in order to save himself and Eva Marie Saint from the evil clutches of their villainous pursuers. When Grant defeats the villains on Mount Rushmore, we watch breathlessly as Eva Marie Saint hangs on for her life on the side of a cliff, while debonair Cary Grant slowly and carefully tries to pull her to safety. "Hold on," he coaxes her. "You can make it." But then the scene switches in midframe, and our hero Grant is now pulling his heroine, who has just become his wife, into the upper berth on a train. All is well as they begin their honeymoon express.

Mel Brooks, parodying Hitchcock, in *High Anxiety*, creates a similar situation when his lovebirds, who happen to be Brooks and Madeleine Kahn, survive inflicted evils of comic villains, and wind up in a cozy honeymoon resort in the Poconos. The film ends with our newly wedded hero and heroine kissing in a heart-shaped pool.

Madeline Kahn and Mel Brooks in "High Anxiety"

For Hollywood moviemakers, honeymoons were, more often than not, a way of ending the movie. They indicated that all went well with love, and the hero and heroine did live happily ever after. It wasn't particularly easy to show the happily-ever-after part because the Hays Commission had made it unlawful to show wedded, as well as unwedded, couples sharing the same bed. Since no one would believe that a honeymooning couple would spend their wedding night in twin beds, a wedding-night scene in the bridal chamber would be shot with the newlyweds sitting on top of a double bed, or one member of the couple in bed and the other about to get in. Of course, when the Hollywood movie codes became more lax, post-Doris Day, anyone could sleep anywhere with anyone they chose, at any given time. Despite the great sexual liberation of our day, the romantic ideals of our society still seem to be based on the movies of the forties and the fifties.

Honeymoons, alone, do not fairly represent the true meaning of marriage, and Hollywood occasionally let us in on the fact that if the spirit of the honeymoon wasn't right, neither was the marriage.

In *Woman of the Year*, Katharine Hepburn plays a brilliant political columnist who falls for sportswriter Spencer Tracy. They marry quickly, in a small southern town. After the ceremony, Hepburn rushes back to New York to make a speech. She then forces Tracy to move into her Park Avenue apartment, where Hepburn's snotty maid treats him like an uninvited guest.

Their wedding night is interrupted by the arrival of Dr. Lubeck, a great scientist, who has escaped from a Nazi concentration camp, and has raced to Hepburn's New York apartment to give her an exclusive on his story. Accompanied by his German-speaking friends, they descend on Hepburn and Tracy's bedroom. Tracy doesn't speak any German, and sits on his wedding bed, clad in bathrobe and pajamas, feeling irritated and bored. Then, in a fit of frustration, Tracy phones up his sports buddies and invites them over for a party in his bedroom. Bedlam in the boudoir ensues. Finally, when they discover that this is Hepburn and Tracy's wedding night, all the unwanted guests leave.

Their marriage is to be continually plagued by similar problems after this episode, though, because Hepburn is too busy with her exciting career to spend time being a wife to Tracy. Tracy finally gets totally fed up and walks out on her. Hepburn realizes her errors and vows to change. Moral of the story: If you don't have time for the honeymoon, you don't have time for the marriage.

Katharine Hepburn and Spencer Tracy in "Woman of the Year"

A honeymoon is put to the test in *High Noon*, when Sheriff Gary Cooper marries Quaker pacifist Grace Kelly and lays down his gun forever. Cooper has given up his job as sheriff in a lawless town only to find himself pursued by a band of killers he had once sent to jail. The killers had subsequently been released from prison and are now seeking their revenge. Kelly wants Cooper to quickly leave town with her, but Cooper refuses because he feels that he will always be running away. He is disappointed in the town he tamed, and saddened to see it return to its lawless ways. He solicits aid from the new sheriff and the townspeople, but they all refuse to become involved.

Grace Kelly and Gary Cooper in "High Noon"

Left to his own devices, he bravely faces the killer gang alone, and single-handedly defeats most of them. Yet at a crucial moment in the big shoot-out, when all seems lost and Cooper's death is imminent, Kelly steps in and shoots the last member of the gang. Moral of the story: In marriage, one must make sacrifices.

♥   ♥   ♥

Ava Gardner spends a bizarre and tragic honeymoon in *The Barefoot Contessa*. As a fairy-tale movie goddess, she shocks all of Hollywood and the world because she refuses to link herself romantically with anyone. She finally finds her prince charming in Rossano Brazzi, who is an Italian count from a distinguished old family. Love-goddess Gardner is at her sexiest on her wedding night, and paces her bedchamber waiting for the dashing Brazzi to sweep her off her feet. Brazzi enters, kisses her on the cheek, asks her to believe that he loves her with all his heart, and then hands her a piece of paper which he says will "explain everything." The letter is a military document attesting to the wounds Brazzi suffered during World War II. The document alludes to the fact that Brazzi is only "half a man." Heartbroken, Ava Gardner decides to save her marriage by providing Brazzi with what he really wants most, a male heir. Brazzi, however, is both proud and jealous. When he discovers Gardner's unfaithfulness, he shoots her. Moral of the story: Sexless honeymoons don't make it.

Hayley Mills and Hywel Bennett in "The Family Way"   Ava Gardner and Rosanno Brazzi in "The Barefoot Contessa"

Another movie that dealt with the actual consummation of marriage was *The Family Way*. The newly married Hywel Bennett is unable to consummate his marriage with his wife, Hayley Mills. They are both virgins, and Mills thinks it's all her fault and feels inadequate. The real problem, as it turns out, is that they have spent their honeymoon in the home of Bennett's bullying father and as a result Bennett has been too inhibited to be able to perform. Moral of the story: It does matter where you go for a honeymoon.

In *Period of Adjustment*, we had the rare opportunity of watching a rather wretched honeymoon in progress. Young Jim Hutton had just married a sweet little ol' southern belle (Jane Fonda). Fonda wailed, screamed, and complained all the way through their honeymoon, and when an exasperated Hutton complained bitterly to his best friend (Tony Franciosa), the friend claimed that Hutton and Fonda were just learning to know one another, and were going through a little period of adjustment. Blissfully, for all us harassed viewers, the adjustment period ended up well for the honeymooners, and this tortuous movie was over.

Jane Fonda and Tony Franciosa in "Period of Adjustment"

In *Chapter Two*, Marsha Mason and James Caan go to the same honeymoon resort where Caan had taken his first wife, who is now dead. He says he brought Mason there because he remembered it as a very lovely place. Their honeymoon is a fiasco because Caan becomes depressed and misses his dead wife. The more Mason tries to help him forget her, the guiltier he becomes. All is finally set right when Caan gets over his problems in his own way. Moral of the story: Perfect honeymoons take time and practice.

Marsha Mason and James Caan in "Chapter Two"

Honeymoons on the Air

Television and radio picked up where the movies left off. In a series of weekly situation comedies we were finally able to hear and witness what happily-ever-after was really all about. The airwaves gave us a daily glimpse of life-long honeymoons. We saw the thrill of romance die and be reborn again with our favorite honeymooning couples.

In the fifties, *The Honeymooners* and *I Love Lucy* set the stage for our perceptions of honeymoons and marriage. Love never died, though the husband and wife could become highly irritated with each other.

Ralph and Alice Kramden (Jackie Gleason and Audrey Meadows) of *The Honeymooners* spent fifteen years of their marriage in a two-room walk-up apartment, whose main room contained only a dining room table and chairs, a chest of drawers, and an antiquated icebox and stove. Ralph Kramden was an overweight, loutish bus driver. He was self-centered, bossy, and impractical. Time and again his harebrained schemes and selfishness led the couple into trouble. Alice was pragmatic, sensible, sarcastic, carping, and also, on occasion, giving and compassionate. But they supported each other. It was a honeymoon at its best and worst.

A typical Kramden dialogue:

RALPH (as Alice is threatening to leave home and go stay with her mother): Just remember, Alice, you can't put your arms around a memory.

ALICE: I can't even put my arms around you!

RALPH (with clenched fist): To the moon, Alice. Bang! Zoom!

Another argument:

RALPH: Alice, when are you going to learn that a marriage is like a ship, and that the husband is captain of the ship? The wife is just a lowly third class seaman. The captain makes the decisions, charts the course, and runs the ship. The seaman simply gets the mess, swabs the deck, and sees to it that the captain is happy. Get that, Alice? Where are you going?

ALICE: (saluting): Seaman Kramden, third class, is retiring to the poop deck until this big wind blows over.

Yet at the end of each show, the Kramdens had resolved their problems. Ralph had recognized his failings, and Alice had forgiven and accepted him. Ralph would throw his arms around Alice and pronounce, "Baby, you're the greatest!"

We never saw the Kramden bedroom. We knew it was there and we could see the doorway to it on our television sets. We merely assumed that they went in there and honeymooned after the show, when the crisis was resolved and they had made up. We also assumed that things went pretty well for them in there. Why else would Alice tolerate Ralph, and why else would these two human beings stay trapped week after week in that crummy one-bedroom apartment? They didn't even have a phone.

Ed Norton (Art Carney), Ralph Kramden (Jackie Gleason) and Alice Kramden (Audrey Meadows)
"The Honeymooners"

Lucy and Ricky Ricardo were more affluent than Ralph and Alice Kramden. Lucille Ball and Desi Arnaz were playing a television parody of their own married lives. When Ms. Ball became pregnant in real life, so did the television Lucy. (In a lucky television programming break, Lucy gave birth to her son Desi, Jr., the same night that the television Lucy had Little Ricky.) Lucy and Ricky were the first television odd couple. They honeymooned through life, even in the face of their basic ethnic and social differences. They were perfect foils for each other: a wacky, innocently scheming redhead, and a Cuban bandleader with a temper. They were sexual dynamite. You could always tell that Ricky did, indeed, love Lucy, as the show's title proclaimed, and their dialogue was filled with "honey" and "sweetheart." The show was also filled with Lucy crying, scheming, and plotting, while Ricky handled it all by swearing in Spanish.

The Ricardo marriage seemed comfortable, a big, life-long honeymoon. This was especially so when it was contrasted to the marriage of Fred and Ethel Mertz, friends and neighbors of the Ricardos. The Mertz marriage was an atrocity. Their honeymoon was long over. It seemed as though they had stayed married only to become a foil for Lucy and Ricky's various shenanigans, or perhaps to collect rent from the couple. It must be noted that perhaps the longest and best honeymoon on television was actually the one between Lucy and Ethel.

Lucy and Ricky Ricardo, (Lucille Ball and Desi Arnaz) "I Love Lucy"

Roy Rodgers, Dale Evans and Trigger

Radio and television comedies portrayed marriage as an eternal battle of the sexes. The major networks competed with one another for good ratings and more advertisers, resulting in many similar formats and practically interchangeable honeymoons and marriages.

When CBS was successful with *I Love Lucy*, NBC created *I Married Joan* (with comedienne Joan Davis as a wacky blonde wife to practical Jim Backus). Old radio comics revamped their material for television, and George Burns continued to honeymoon with his real wife, dizzy Gracie Allen; and Mary Livingstone, with her real-life hubby, penny-pinching Jack Benny.

Real-life marrieds Roy Rogers and Dale Evans changed the pace for us by honeymooning on horseback, catching bad guys and bringing them to justice, and singing "Happy Trails to You." Bandleader Ozzie Nelson and his real wife, Harriet Hilliard, honeymooned on the *Ozzie and Harriet Show*, with their two real-life sons, David and Ricky. They became the symbol of perfect family life in America.

Happy honeymooning ghouls: "The Munsters" (left) and "Bewitched"

The television moguls used the marriage formula over and over.

Then in a halfhearted attempt to prevent too much repetition, they began offering us marriages with a twist. In *Biff Baker*, the honeymooning couple worked as undercover agents inside the Soviet Union. TV also revamped the old *Thin Man* series from the movies. The happily married Nick and Nora Charles were private eyes who simultaneously battled crime and solved their own domestic crises.

Jackie Cooper secretly married Patricia Breslin in *The People's Choice*, and only Cleo, the talking dog, knew about the covert honeymoon. In *December Bride* the center of attention was Spring Byington, who played a wacky-wise-wonderful old widow who advises and meddles in the new marriage of her daughter.

In still more attempts to keep the subject fresh, they created some bizarre situations for love and marriage. A mortal unwittingly marries a witch in *Bewitched*. The witch has agreed to give up her craft, except occasionally, when she doesn't feel like doing the dishes. Then she will simply twist her nose and the dishes are shiny clean in the dish drainer. An astronaut finds an old bottle, in *I Dream of Jeannie*. He rubs the bottle and a female genie appears, who is beautiful and totally devoted to him. He marries her, and she makes magic for him, though he continually begs her not to, because he wants to lead a normal existence. In *Room for One More*, the honeymooning couple is continually adopting new children, making this series as unbelievable as *I Dream of Jeannie*.

Then there were *The Addams Family* and *The Munsters*, or more aptly, honeymoons among the monsters. Needless to say, while all these marriages were somehow problematical, they were nonetheless happy.

♥   ♥   ♥

In the early seventies there was a long-overdue renaissance in television situation comedies. In *All in the Family*, we watched Archie Bunker repeatedly disapprove of his daughter Gloria's marriage to Mike Stivic, because Stivic was Polish and politically liberal. The Bunkers and the Stivics battled it out for eight amusing years, and then to our horror, but not our surprise, the Stiviks got divorced.

Mike Stivic (Rob Reiner), Gloria Stivic (Sally Struthers) in "All In The Family"

We celebrated when once-overweight, neurotic Rhoda Morgenstern married Joe. (Their honeymoon, a wedding present from her overly protective parents was a Caribbean cruise on a luxury liner. Unfortunately their cabin was too small for both of them, and the other clientele of the boat most nearly resembled a geriatrics ward. They jumped ship in Baltimore.)

At this point in our now-sophisticated television lives, we took it in stride when Joe walked out on Rhoda a few years later. Divorce had become a way of life on television, and Joe was boring anyway.

Rhoda marries Joe in "Rhoda"

The agony and ecstasy of life came our way at prime-time hours via *Peyton Place*. We got to watch Rodney Harrington get Betty Anderson pregnant, then dump her for Alison MacKenzie. Then we watched Betty marry someone else when we all knew that she was still in love with Rodney. We watched Betty's honeymoon, clucking our tongues and saying, "We know she'll never be happy with him. It won't last."

For all us honeymoon voyeurs there was nothing more uplifting and gratifying than *The Newlywed Game*. Daily, we had the opportunity of watching newlywed couples test the appropriateness of their match on a slick TV quiz show. The honeymooners who knew each other the best would deservedly win big cash prizes or new cars. The other less familiar honeymooners would walk away with lowly toaster ovens, or a year's supply of popcorn.

The game worked like this. Three husbands would be paraded on stage and asked questions about their wives' tastes. (The wives were kept out of earshot.) The master of ceremonies would ask each husband the same list of questions, such as, "The car my wife would most like to own is a _____?"

After the husbands had answered these tricky questions, the wives would be paraded before all of television land and asked to respond to the same questions. If their answers matched the ones given by the husband, the honeymooners would win points, which would later be exchanged for fabulous cash prizes.

More often than not, there would be a couple who continually gave opposing answers. "Honeeey," the wife would say with irritation, "I never said that."

"Yes, you did," the husband would counter. "You just don't remember."

The success or failure in the viewers' pleasure of this game show was largely dependent on how irritated the respective spouses became with each other. The master of ceremonies seemed to take pride in the amount of damage he could inflict on the diverse honeymooners, all within a half-hour time slot.

The damage, of course, was never very serious. By the end of the show, all the couples were happy, even the losers, who kissed and made up. They offered us the hope that honeymoons could really last forever.

Honeymoon Heaven on the air?

CHAPTER SEVEN

A HONEYMOON WHO'S WHO

Since we all believe that the rich and beautiful people lead rich and beautiful lives, it would follow that most of them had rich and beautiful honeymoons! If you had yachts and castles at your fingertips, would you have settled for a few kisses at Niagara Falls or a weekend at the Waldorf?

Here's a look at the real-life (and sometimes rich and beautiful) honeymoons of our larger-than-life heroes.

● ● ●

● The Honeymoon of Catherine the Great and Peter III ●

Her name wasn't Catherine, and she wasn't even Russian. Elizabeth II, Empress of Russia, had handpicked an obscure German princess named Sophia to be the wife of her nephew, the Grand Duke Peter III, heir to the throne of imperial Russia.

Though young Sophia's family was of lesser royalty, Sophia was selected for the throne because she was well educated, healthy, attractive, and from all appearances, the perfect candidate for the bearing of healthy male heirs. The Russian Empire desperately needed healthy heirs. Elizabeth, who was an intelligent and strong ruler, was childless (though hardly virginal), and her nephew Peter was, at best, irresponsible and immature, and at worst, totally demented.

The young Sophia, whose name was subsequently changed to Catherine because it sounded more Russian, was brought to the Kremlin with her mother, taught fluent Russian, and educated thoroughly in tsarist court etiquette. Peter thought the German princess was brought to court as a new playmate for him. He proudly displayed and paraded all his toy soldiers before her.

Catherine watched as her mother fell from grace with the Empress Elizabeth. She looked on as the German mother was sent home in disgrace and poverty shortly after Catherine's marriage to the grand duke. Catherine was to spend her first years of marriage alone and friendless in a strange land, often endangered by the bizarre politics of the Kremlin court.

Catherine was finally married to Peter in 1745. She was fifteen and a half years old. Peter was nearly seventeen. The wedding was a great national event, staged by Elizabeth. The empress was very concerned with her country's international prestige, and modeled the wedding festivities after the customary ceremonies at the court of Versailles.

Catherine wore a shimmering silver bridal gown, which was covered with silver embroidery and a cloak of silver lace. She was practically smothered in exquisite jewels. The groom's attire was completely white.

The wedding ceremony took place in Kazan Cathedral. Catherine later remembered it as "one long, painful ordeal." A procession of twenty carriages, all with gilded wheels, and each drawn by six white horses, wended their way to the cathedral. The oppressed and impoverished townspeople lined the streets to cheer this opulent parade, while powdered-wigged footmen kicked the people out of the path of the carriages.

The bride and groom rode together in Empress Elizabeth's golden carriage. The bride's mother was reduced to the humiliation of following in a lowly back carriage. The bride's father was not even invited to the wedding.

Catherine's exhaustion during this ordeal was largely due to the fact that she had to endure the procession, the hour-long ceremony, and a court ball in her silver wedding attire—the equivalent of spending the entire day in a suit of armor.

Catherine did somehow manage to enjoy herself at the wedding ball, if briefly. She danced with many young handsome men of the empress's court. But this did not go unnoticed by Elizabeth, who ushered her to her bridal chamber after only a half hour of dancing.

The procession to Catherine's bridal chamber rivaled the procession to her wedding ceremony. In order, the procession included Elizabeth, the master of ceremonies, the grand master of the court, the grand marshal, the grand chamberlain of the grand duke's court, Catherine herself, Peter, the princess mother, the Princess of Hesse, the grand mistress, and three ladies-in-waiting. It seemed more like a funeral procession than a honeymoon.

Once the ladies were in full attendance, the men left the nuptial chamber and returned to the ball.

The bride was undressed by her ladies-in-waiting, and the Empress Elizabeth removed Catherine's crown. Catherine was dressed in her nightclothes by the Princess of Hesse, and the grand mistress administered the dressing gown. The bride was instructed to climb into bed, and once so situated, all the grandes dames marched out of the chamber.

Suddenly young Catherine was left alone with all her fears in a bedchamber of scarlet velvet. She shivered nervously in her elaborate silver-inlaid wedding bed. She waited there for two hours while her new husband failed to appear.

The idiot groom Peter was in no hurry to enter the marriage chamber. He remained at the ball, and later went into the kitchen looking for his supper. He, too, was understandably nervous and frightened, but he had no desire or intention of fulfilling his marriage functions. He still considered Catherine his playmate.

Peter finally succumbed to exhaustion and entered the nuptial chamber with his arms laden with toy soldiers. He laid them out on the bed to make a display for Catherine. He spent the rest of his wedding night talking about his toys and his favorite games, while an exhausted Catherine feigned interest. They did not consummate their marriage that night, nor for seven years of nights to come.

Despite the physical defects of the wedding night, the newly married grand duke and duchess spent their honeymoon hiding their boredom at an array of court festivities. They were showered with presents, and attended balls, fireworks displays, masquerades, and ridiculously opulent parades in their honor. In the evening, Catherine would yawn while Peter continued to parade his toy soldiers on their wedding bed. During their so-called honeymoon, Catherine's only real pleasure came from long talks with her mother.

The Empress Elizabeth soon caught on to the charade in the nuptial chamber, and exiled Catherine's mother. She blamed Catherine for not arousing the grand duke to consummate his marriage.

The grand duke soon became involved in organizing a royal puppet theater, which Catherine considered to be "the most insipid thing in the world." When the thrill of the puppet theater wore off, the duke found pleasure in drilling peepholes into the various boudoirs of the palace. He had great fun spying on everyone. Eventually, his hand drill wound its way into the boudoir of the empress, and Peter had the pleasure of spying on his Aunt Elizabeth's many and varied affairs. Peter forced Catherine into a clandestine peek, but Catherine refused to have any further part in this.

Fortunately for Catherine, when the duke was caught and subsequently punished for his transgressions, she could proclaim total innocence. But she had learned a lot when she invaded the empress's privacy. Shortly thereafter, she began her own affairs, bore Russia an illegitimate heir, and lived to become Empress Catherine the Great.

♥ ♥ ♥

♥ The Honeymoon of George and Martha Washington ♥

George Washington never told a lie. He once said, "Love may and ought to be under the guidance of reason," and he followed his own advice.

As a young colonel in colonial America, Washington had found himself madly infatuated with Sally Fairfax, who was married to a man she didn't love. The society of the day prevented her from divorcing him. Washington viewed the whole situation as impossible for him. Though he fantasized about running off with Sally Fairfax, he was too much the pragmatist to allow himself to live in social exile, ruin his military career, and defame his mistress.

So he gave the whole matter up. He felt the ache of disappointment, but lacked the courage to fight for the woman he loved. Instead, he considered his future, and decided that it behooved him to find a wealthy, socially acceptable mate.

"Under the guidance of reason," he focused his attentions on a rather plain but wealthy widow named Martha Custis. Martha's family were respectable Virginia landowners, and though she was no longer young, Martha was a serious, patient woman who seemed to be a perfect potential wife for a career soldier.

Washington proposed marriage shortly after their first meeting, and Mrs. Custis, who was equally as pragmatic, decided it looked like a good deal.

They were married on January 6, 1759, at St. Peter's Church in New Kent County, near the Custis family home. Polite Virginia society attended the predictable and unmemorable wedding ceremony. Martha wore a wedding dress of quilted white silk and satin. She allowed herself to display a little of her family's wealth by arriving at the wedding ceremony in a carriage drawn by six white horses.

The newlyweds honeymooned through the winter in fashionable Williamsburg, and returned to Washington's plantation, Mount Vernon, in the summer.

One regrets noting that George Washington probably displayed more passion at Valley Forge than he did at Williamsburg.

♥   ♥   ♥

♥ A Jazz-Baby Honeymoon: ♥
The Honeymoon of F. Scott and Zelda Fitzgerald

He was the darling of the New York literary set. His first novel, *This Side of Paradise*, was about to be published and catapult him to fame, though never fortune. His lifestyle would make him legendary, and *The Great Gatsby* would make him immortal.

She was an old-time southern belle who was well educated and flip and sarcastic. Later she would become a beacon of twenties style, and a symbol of the great cabaret life.

Scottie had said that he was marrying the prettiest girl in Georgia and Alabama. His friends thought not. The impression Zelda made among Scottie's New York cronies was of a spoiled, old-fashioned, small-town southern belle. She was overly temperamental, sulky, and harsh and showed her knees when no one wanted to see them. They also thought her somewhat mentally unbalanced, and they were right.

Scottie and Zelda were married on April 3, 1920, in the rectory of St. Patrick's Cathedral in New York. Zelda wore a suit of midnight blue and a matching hat trimmed with buckles and ribbons. She carried a bouquet of orchids and white flowers. The wedding ceremony was brief and uneventful, and the wedding party was composed of an intimate group of close friends.

The bride and groom spent their wedding night and honeymoon in Suite 2109 of the Biltmore Hotel. Arriving in chic New York, Zelda felt dowdy and frumpy, and spent the first day of her honeymoon shopping for new clothes. She had a good eye for style, and instantly turned herself into the public's idea of a "Jazz Baby."

They lived high at the Biltmore, on Scottie's advance money from his publisher. They invited their friends to drop in at the honeymoon suite. The friends often arrived to find the newlyweds jovially drinking champagne in the bathtub. Of course, the friends were invited into the bathroom to join them. The bathtub scenes would sometimes become rowdy, and temperamental Zelda became uncontainable when tipsy. The friends would then have the pleasure (or disappointment) of witnessing a huge, soggy row in the postnuptial tub.

The Fitzgeralds' honeymoon antics were a prelude to the free-wheeling roaring twenties, and possibly a prelude to the heart-shaped tubs of the Poconos, as well.

SCOTTIE

ZELDA

2109

KAREN KATZ

• The Honeymoon of Ike and Mamie Eisenhower •

Dwight D. Eisenhower was a born American hero. He selected his heroine early in life, and his choice was impeccable. Mamie Dowd was pretty and popular and came from a family with just enough money. They were, from the start, the perfect "presidential couple."

Ike married Mamie in her father's custom-built Victorian mansion in Denver, Colorado, on July 1, 1916. It was a nice, Presbyterian ceremony, followed by a simple reception, and attended by the friends and family of the Dowds. In a "shucks-gee whiz" manner, Ike had bought Mamie a wedding ring for seventy dollars. By astonishing coincidence, Ike received notification of his appointment as first lieutenant on his wedding day. There was much cause for celebration.

Mamie, dressed in a traditional white lace wedding gown, was solemnly and proudly given away by her father. Ike wore his tropical white dress uniform. He was so concerned with his ability to cut a dashing figure that he refused to sit down during the wedding reception, so that he might preserve the freshly pressed creases in his white trousers.

With a great show of all-American bravura, Ike cut the wedding cake with his sword, and the wedding guests applauded.

After the reception, Ike whisked Mamie away to El Dorado Springs for a brief, but happy, weekend honeymoon. Then the newlyweds set off for Abilene, Texas, to meet with Ike's family. Mamie, of course, easily won all the Eisenhower hearts, and the couple was showered with wedding gifts and attention.

Pleased with Mamie's success with his family, Ike guiltlessly deposited her in Abilene, and went off on a two-week army maneuver. It was to be the first of many separations. Mamie never complained.

♥   ♥   ♥

• The Honeymoon of Rudolph Valentino and Jean Acker •

At the time, he called himself Rudolpho di Valentine. He was an Italian immigrant, making his way in Hollywood by playing bit parts and working as an extra. *The Four Horsemen of the Apocalypse*, and instant fame, were a year and a half away.

He met Jean Acker at a Hollywood party. She was a successful working actress at Metro, and young Rudolpho admired her Metro salary and fancy Hollywood address. Ms. Acker took a flattered interest in the future great screen lover. She suggested that he change his name to Rudolph Valentino.

He did. Over a single weekend he courted her, and impulsively asked her to marry him. Acker accepted. Perhaps she did so out of amusement, because Valentino always tried to play the great lover off camera. Acker thought simply that Rudolph Valentino was very silly. Though understandable why she accepted Valentino's proposal, it is difficult to fathom why she bothered to go through with the marriage.

They had a small wedding at the Hollywood Hotel, and a simple supper immediately after the wedding service. Only a few close friends attended the modest festivities. Valentino and Acker had planned to spend their wedding night at the Hollywood Hotel.

After the guests departed, Acker permitted Valentino to hold her hand as they walked toward their bridal chamber. Valentino inserted the key into the door lock, and Acker smiled as he opened the door. Then, just as Valentino was preparing to lift his bride over the threshold, she skipped into the room and slammed the door in his face.

Valentino laughed. He assumed this was simply a merry prank from a shy bride. He banged on the door, but to his horror, he heard Acker fasten the safety lock. He banged again, with desperation. Finally she told him to go away. She didn't want to see him, because the marriage had been "a terrible mistake." She further declared that she had married him out of pity, that she did not love him, that she wanted to be his friend but not his wife.

Valentino could not believe this rejection. He continued to pound on the door, but there soon ceased to be any response. His amusement had turned to fury, and then to depression. He dismally raced out of the hotel into the street, where he threw up his wedding dinner.

Valentino was ashamed. To him there was nothing more degrading or insulting than to be locked out of his own wedding chamber. In the days following he made desperate attempts to contact Acker at the hotel, but she refused to take his phone calls. Several days later she left the hotel to stay with a friend, and made no attempt to get in touch with her new husband.

Valentino doggedly continued to pursue his bride. Finally, at his wits' end, he wrote her this letter:

My Dear Jean,

I am at a complete loss to understand your conduct towards me, as I cannot receive any satisfactory explanation through telephoning or seeing you.

Since I cannot force my presence upon you, either at the hotel, or at Grace's, where you spend most of your time, I guess I'd better give it up. I am always ready to furnish you a home and all the comfort to the best of my modest means and ability, as well as all the love and care of a husband for his dear little wife.

Please, Jean, darling, come to your senses and give me an opportunity to prove my sincere love and eternal devotion to you.

Your unhappy loving husband,
Rudolpho

♥ ♥ ♥

Several weeks passed and Valentino received no reply. Acker had left her friend's home and gone on location with a Metro film crew to begin shooting a new movie. A month after his letter, Valentino received this telegram:

I CANNOT PROMISE TO VISIT YOU CHRISTMAS STOP HEARTBROKEN BUT WORK BEFORE PLEASURE STOP BE A GOOD BOY STOP REMEMBER ME EVERY SECOND STOP—JEAN

♥ ♥ ♥

When Rudolph Valentino divorced Jean Acker a year later, their marriage was still unconsummated.

● The Honeymoon of the Duke and Duchess of Windsor ●

It was, perhaps, one of the most unpopular honeymoons in British history. King Edward VIII had abdicated his throne for the woman he loved. He had been the popular Prince Edward, Prince of Wales, heir to the throne, beloved by his subjects. He would have been the golden liege, as he was the golden prince. Yet, he gave up the throne to marry Wallis Warfield Simpson, an American citizen and a commoner, who had been twice divorced. This was the greatest love story of the twentieth century.

They planned a "quiet" wedding. The British press had agreed to ignore it, as they did not want to stir up the rage of the British public, who were already incensed at the abdication.

They were married on June 3, 1937, in the small town of Condé, in southern France. Only a few close friends were invited to the wedding, but the crowd of onlookers and international reporters numbered at least a thousand.

Mrs. Simpson wore a blue silk crepe dress, designed for her by Schiaparelli, who also designed Mrs. Simpson's entire trousseau. The two-piece gown, with a long clinging skirt, was copied by American dress designers as soon as the wedding pictures hit the States. The British press treated this wedding as an ordinary social event, so the dress did not make it to the racks of Harrods.

The bride was very concerned with proper tradition and wore something old (antique lace stitched to her lingerie), something new (a gold coin minted for Edward VIII's coronation, which she slipped inside her left shoe), something borrowed (a handkerchief), and something blue (her wedding gown).

After the ceremony, the couple celebrated their marriage at a breakfast reception. They then hopped a train to Venice, and fed pigeons in the Piazza San Marco. Soon they were off to their honeymoon retreat on an Alpine peak.

Edward had investigated seventy old castles for his "simple" honeymoon. He settled on Wasselerleonburg Castle, built in the thirteenth century, which was isolated on a mountain top and surrounded by lakes. The castle was attended to by a horde of servants, and the bride and groom were able to honeymoon under maximum security protection.

They arrived at their castle by limousine, along with their two hundred and sixty-six pieces of luggage. Edward gallantly managed to carry his bride over the threshold, with only a slight stumble.

With a sense of tradition befitting their thirteenth-century castle retreat, the bride and groom drank honey for the time of the full moon. They spent the rest of their honeymoon (about three weeks) taking long walks together and climbing mountains. Their evenings they spent quietly alone, rehashing the horrors of the abdication.

♥ The Real-Life Honeymoon of Lucille Ball and Desi Arnaz ♥

Desi met Lucy on the RKO movie set of *Too Many Girls*, where Lucy played an ingenue to Desi's leading man. A volatile, rocky romance sprang up between the two stars almost immediately after their first meeting. When their movie was finished, Desi went back to New York to star in Broadway musicals, and Lucy stayed on with RKO to make more movies.

Lucy traveled to New York to promote one of her RKO movies, and Desi, unhappy about how much time they were spending apart, insisted that they get married. On November 30, 1940, the couple got up at 6:00 A.M. and drove from New York to a small town in Connecticut for their wedding ceremony. Desi had hoped to be wed in the morning, and then return to New York for his matinee performance. Desi convinced the probate judge to waive the five-day wait for a marriage license, but the judge insisted that the couple pass a Wasserman test. So Desi and Lucy hopped in their car and drove around Connecticut looking for a general practitioner who would administer the test in a hurry. They found one, passed their tests, and rushed back to the justice of the peace at the Bryan River Beagle Club for the ceremony. Desi still had time to make his matinee.

Unfortunately, when the couple and the best man were finally assembled in front of the justice of the peace, Desi realized he had forgotten to buy a wedding ring. The best man volunteered to run out and buy one while Lucy and Desi waited at the altar. All the local jewelry stores were closed, though, and the best man came back empty-handed. Finally, Desi went out and bought a ring at the five and ten cent store. Lucy loved it, and continued to wear it for years.

At the end of the wedding ceremony, it was apparent that Desi was going to miss his matinee performance. He phoned the theater and arranged for his stand-in to go on in his place. The theater management congratulated him on his marriage, and were relieved to find that he would make it back to New York in time for his evening performance.

Desi and Lucy drove back to New York without mishap, and the groom carried his bride over the threshold of his dressing room.

Before the curtain went up, the theater manager announced the marriage of Desi Arnaz to Lucille Ball. Lucy and Desi were ushered onto the stage to waves of applause, and pelted with rice by the theater audience (the management having cleverly handed out packets of rice to the audience as they were being seated).

After the show, the cast at the Roxy held a party for the newlyweds at El Morocco. Champagne flowed like a river, and the exhausted and tipsy honeymooners were glad to slip away to their nuptial chamber at the Hotel Pierre. (Their room was provided for them by RKO.)

A drunken Desi woke up thirsty in the middle of the night. He roused Lucy and demanded she bring him a glass of water. Lucy sleepily agreed, got up, brought him the water, and went back to sleep.

The next morning, Desi awoke to Lucy's fury. She would never again get up and get him water in the middle of the night. She insisted that he do it himself, and that he had no business waking her. For the rest of their marriage, a water pitcher and glass were kept on Desi's night table.

Another postnuptial crisis arose over the room temperature. Desi kept closing the window and Lucy kept opening it. Desi insists that he spent his entire marriage to Lucy half frozen.

Several days later, the newlyweds boarded a train for a three-day honeymoon trip back to California. Desi passed the time by strumming on his guitar and composing this honeymoon song for Lucy.

When I looked into your eyes
And then you softly said "I do"
I suddenly realized that I had a new world
A world with you
A world where life is worth living
A world that is so new to me

A world of taking and giving
Like God meant the world to be
Where good times will find two to greet
Where hard times will find two to beat
I found my new world with you, darling,
When you softly said, "I do."

The melody of the song became the *I Love Lucy* theme song. Each year on their anniversary Desi would sing the song to Lucy and bring her red and white carnations.

It has been nearly two decades since their divorce. But Desi still sends Lucy red and white carnations on their anniversary.

♥ The Honeymoon of Jean Harlow and Paul Bern ♥

They were a Hollywood odd couple. Harlow was a major star, a love goddess, a fine comedienne on her way to becoming a fine actress. She was as outgoing and vivacious as she was attractive. Paul Bern, a successful producer, was cultivated, aesthetic, modest, quiet, and introverted.

They met on the set of *Red-Headed Woman*, which starred Harlow and was produced by Bern. Harlow had later stated that Bern was attracted to her thoughts, and that their relationship was intellectual.

Their marriage plans shocked all of Hollywood. The gossip columnists called it a "ludicrous" match. Rumors had circulated about Bern's alleged impotence, and Harlow was known to be sexually dynamic. Before the wedding ceremony, Harlow heard the Bern rumors. She cried for several days, said she didn't believe them, and then decided that she didn't care whether or not they were true. She was resolved to go ahead with the wedding.

They were married on July 2, 1932, at the home of Jean's mother. The ceremony was performed by Superior Judge Leon Yankwich. It was a small ceremony with only a few close friends in attendance. John Gilbert stood as best man.

THE HOLLYWOOD REPORTER, OCTOBER 24, 1950

FLYNNS' FLEE ABOARD YACHT ZACA

Film idol Errol Flynn aboard his yacht Zaca, fending off an over-zealous fan as his new bride, debutante Patrice Wymore looks on.

Special to The Reporter

MONTE CARLO, Oct. 23 — In the early morning hours dare-devil film idol Errol Flynn, aided by a close friend, one Prince Umberto, lived up to his reputation as a swashbuckling Hollywood he-man as he fled Monaco police through a hotel casino clad only in his pajamas to the delight and amusement of all-night gamblers.

NANCY GREENBERG

The next day the newlyweds threw an elaborate reception at Bern's home, a two-story European mansion, complete with the swimming pool he had given to Harlow as a wedding present.

The bride was in the middle of filming another picture at the time of her marriage and could not get away for a honeymoon. Bern would visit Harlow daily on the set, but after several weeks the newlyweds were seen arguing.

On September 6, 1932, two months after their wedding, Paul Bern shot himself in the head. This suicide note was left on the night table near his body:

Dearest Jean,
Unfortunately, this is the only way to make good the frightful wrong I've
done you, and to wipe out my abject humility. I love you.
                    P.S. You understand that last night was only a comedy.

Next to the note was a publicity photograph of Harlow.

● ● ●

• The Honeymoon of Errol Flynn and Patrice Wymore •

Errol Flynn was the last of the dashing and swashbuckling Hollywood he-men. His third marriage was to Patrice Wymore, debutante, beauty, ingenue, and sometime actress.

Wymore's wealthy family were ready to embrace dare-devil Flynn as their son-in-law, but not without reservations, which were about to prove justified. Wymore and Flynn had planned a wedding in Monaco, with Prince Rainier in attendance. Flynn's wedding day, October 23, 1950, was declared a national holiday there.

On October 22, a young girl who worked in a perfume shop and her irate father went to the Monte Carlo police and accused Errol Flynn of rape. The girl was only sixteen, and statutory rape carried a heavy penalty in Monaco.

On the morning of his wedding day, the police cautiously surrounded Flynn's hotel, preparing for his arrest. Prince Umberto, a close friend of Flynn's, had heard about the rape charge. He sneaked into Flynn's room and warned him.

Flynn and Umberto planned a daring escape. Still clad in his pajamas, Flynn, accompanied by the prince, crept down the hotel stairway to an underground tunnel adjoining the casino. Flynn's flight through the casino in his pajamas caused great laughter among the all-night gamblers, and the straggling crowd cheered him on as he and the prince made a valiant escape through an open window.

They jumped from the casino window to a garden and made a mad dash to their car. From there they sped to a motorboat, which took them to Flynn's yacht, *Zaca*. Once aboard the yacht, they sailed out to the free-water zone.

The tale of Flynn's daring escape circulated through the hotel and was met with great amusement. The police were so entertained by all this that they decided to drop the charge. Flynn was radioed on his yacht that all was forgiven, and he returned to shore to proceed with his wedding plans.

All of Monte Carlo celebrated Flynn's wedding. After the civil ceremony, conducted by the mayor, the newlyweds whisked themselves away to

Nice for a Lutheran ceremony. The happy couple then returned to Monte Carlo for the wedding reception.

Suddenly, in the middle of a glittering marriage dinner, the Monaco police appeared and arrested Flynn for statutory rape. It seemed that while Flynn was somewhere between Nice and Monte Carlo, the police has lost their sense of humor.

After a long and arduous ordeal at the Monte Carlo police headquarters, Flynn was allowed to enjoy the rest of his wedding night, released on bail.

Mr. and Mrs. Flynn fled to his yacht, racing through crowds of curiosity seekers. Just as Flynn had successfully managed to push his way through the crowd, he slipped on the wet floor of the speedboat and landed flat on his back. His pain was immense. He had smashed a vertebra, and the local doctor ordered him to spend a month in bed. During his month-long recuperation in Monte Carlo, his lawyers met with him at his bedside to prepare for his defense in the rape case.

The prosecution's evidence was sketchy at best, and inconclusive. (Besides, the young perfumist had hairy legs, and it was a well-known fact that Flynn never touched women with hair on their legs.) Flynn was proved innocent of the rape charge, and the case was over.

Two months after their wedding, Flynn and his bride were finally ready to begin their honeymoon. They planned a brief voyage to Spain aboard *Zaca*. Unfortunately, most of their cruise was through gale winds and storm, and when the weather-beaten honeymooners finally hit the Spanish coast, they were too exhausted for any sightseeing.

So they packed their bags and flew back to Hollywood, where Flynn retired to a hospital to undergo physical therapy for his back trouble. The only bright light on the horizon for the newlyweds was the fact that an old paternity suit against Flynn had finally been dropped.

• The Two Honeymoons of Jacqueline Lee Bouvier Kennedy Onassis •

Honeymoon Number One—"Joe Kennedy's Wedding"

Jacqueline Lee Bouvier was married to John Fitzgerald Kennedy on September 12, 1953, at Hammersmith Farm, the estate of Jackie's stepfather, Hugh Auchincloss, in Newport, Rhode Island. She had met John, then the junior senator from Massachusetts, while working as a roving reporter and photographer for a Washington newspaper.

Rumor had it that Jackie had immediately set her cap for young John Kennedy, telling her friends, "He would be a fool not to marry me." John Kennedy was widely believed to be the best catch in Washington, D.C.

Joseph Kennedy, John's ambitious father, was thrilled by the match. The Auchinclosses were one of America's oldest families, and Jackie, through her mother's remarriage, was a member of high society and the American aristocracy. Despite Joe Kennedy's great wealth, the elder Kennedy had found the doors of the "best" American families closed to him. The Kennedy family was Boston, Irish Catholic, political (Joe Kennedy had been an American ambassador to the Court of St. James), but not as yet socially accepted by the older, more established dynasties of American wealth.

Joe Kennedy had big ambitions for his children. He wanted the Presidency of the United States for his oldest surviving son. John Kennedy was well aware of his father's aspirations and had no intention of disappointing him.

Jacqueline Bouvier suited all Joe Kennedy's requirements for the perfect future presidential wife. First and foremost, Jackie was Catholic, and it was imperative that John Kennedy have a Catholic wife if he was to be successfully elected President. Second, Jackie's family ties were invaluable to Joe Kennedy. He sensed that new social and business contacts would emerge as a result of the marriage. Third, Jackie was pretty enough to be a presentable First Lady to the American public and the world. Finally, she was obviously well educated and intelligent, but she was also shy and soft spoken, which meant that she wouldn't offend anyone.

It has always been customary for the bride's family to plan the wedding, and Jackie's mother, Janet Auchincloss, had envisioned a modest ceremony and reception. She found out very quickly, however, that Joe Kennedy had very definite and very different ideas about the forthcoming wedding ceremony and reception. Joe Kennedy wanted to host an extravaganza worthy of the front page of *The New York Times*. Where Mrs. Auchincloss wanted to keep the guest list small and invite only family and a few close friends, Joe Kennedy invited movie stars, political columnists, society reporters, members of Congress, and the Speaker of the House.

As the guest list grew, Janet Auchincloss realized that Joe Kennedy would have his way with this wedding, as he did with most other things in his life. The elder Kennedy arranged for police lines and press coverage. He also saw to it that the wedding ceremony was orthodoxly Catholic. He brought in Cardinal Cushing as celebrant and Monsignor Francis Rossiter as assistant. Then he brought in four more priests to assist the cardinal and the monsignor.

NEIL FLEWELLEN

He even arranged for Pope Pius XII to bless the bride and groom. Joe Kennedy wanted everything to be right with God.

Jackie was oblivous to all this. She was busy buying her trousseau at wholesale outlets. Her only wish for the wedding plans was that her real father, Black Jack Bouvier, would escort her down the aisle and give her away. Her wish highly irritated Janet Auchincloss, who feared that Bouvier, an alcoholic, would in some way embarrass the family.

Janet proved to be right. Bouvier was dead drunk on Jackie's wedding day. He was subsequently taken away from his hotel in an ambulance. Jackie was distraught at the news and wept all morning. She genuinely loved her father, and his presence was very important to her.

Hugh Auchincloss gave the bride away in Newport. The reception went off without a hitch. Joe Kennedy could not have been more pleased.

Jackie's wedding gown was of ivory tissue silk, and her veil was a family heirloom of rose point lace. John Kennedy, who had always been notably disinterested in clothes, had ordered his wedding attire from the Rockefeller family tailor at H. Harris and Company. He had his favorite barber flown to Newport from New York, and was even persuaded to wear a formal top hat for the occasion.

After the wedding reception, Jackie threw her bouquet and garter to her wedding guests, and then John Kennedy whisked her away to a honeymoon in Acapulco, Mexico.

The newlyweds honeymooned in Acapulco for three happy weeks, in a pink villa overlooking the ocean. Jackie would later remember this as the magical time of their marriage. They were totally alone, a luxury they would not enjoy again for a long time. (Later, Jackie would ask her second husband to buy a villa in Acapulco, overlooking the ocean.)

Jackie wrote a compassionate letter to her father forgiving him for his failure to show up for her wedding. After the newlyweds' stay in Mexico, they departed for California to visit some of John's old Navy buddies. Then it was back to the family compound in Hyannisport, and politics as usual.

The Greek Tycoon

The Kennedy family had tried to talk her out of it. The press cried, "Jackie, how could you?" But Jackie Kennedy, widow of a martyred President and the most famous and admired woman in the world, decided to marry Aristotle Onassis, a short, Greek shipping magnate, of Greek Orthodox faith, questionable morals, and a shady business background, twenty years her senior, and one of the wealthiest men in the world.

Jackie had once said, "The American public will forgive me anything, except maybe, running off with Eddie Fisher." Now she was about to do the equivalent by marrying Onassis.

When the news leaked to the press of their impending marriage, Jackie and Onassis decided to step up their wedding plans in order to cut short the public's fury over their match. Onassis had said, "Jackie needs privacy, and I can give it to her."

He sent a private plane from his company, Olympic Airways, for

NEIL FLEWELLEN

Jackie's wedding entourage, which consisted of Jackie's children by Kennedy, her sister, Lee, and several loyal Kennedy sisters.

The plane landed on the Greek isle of Skorpios, which Onassis owned. He had hired two large helicopters, equipped with bullhorns and guns, to guard the island. Unlike Jackie's first wedding ceremony, this one was very private.

On October 20, 1968, Jackie and Ari Onassis were married in a Greek Orthodox ceremony. Jackie wore a long-sleeved two-piece dress of beige chiffon lace, a matching ribbon in her hair, and beige low-heeled shoes. Onassis wore a baggy, blue double-breasted suit, a white shirt, and a red tie.

The ceremony was brief. Afterward, the wedding party was ushered into jeeps and driven to Onassis' yacht, the *Christina,* for the wedding celebration.

The guests marveled at the opulence of the yacht, and then everyone retired to private bedrooms. Later, before dinner was served, Jackie emerged from her nuptial chamber freshly decked out in her new wedding presents from Ari. She wore a huge ring with a cabochon ruby surrounded by dozens of diamonds. Her earrings were dangling ruby hearts decorated with tiny diamonds. The estimated value of these wedding gifts was one million two hundred thousand dollars.

At the wedding dinner Ari presented Jackie with still another gift—a mammoth gold bracelet with a ram's-head design. The ram's head was studded with rubies. It was all a small price to pay for marriage to the most famous woman in the world.

The wedding guests were flabbergasted with Onassis' wealth and generosity, but Jackie took it all in stride. The next day, the guests were all flown back to their various homes, courtesy of Olympic Airways. Onassis flew off to Athens for a business meeting, and Jackie stayed on the yacht with the servants. She phoned her decorator and made plans for the redesigning of her new house on the island of Skorpios. She was certainly a long way from Acapulco.

♥   ♥   ♥

• The Honeymoon of Rita Hayworth and Ali Khan •

It was the world's most expensive honeymoon.

At the time, she was the reigning love goddess in Hollywood. She had just divorced her second husband, Orson Welles, but her public still adored her.

Ali Khan was the son of the Aga Khan, and heir to an Arabian fortune. They met while vacationing in Havana, Cuba. When they both sailed to Europe on the *Britannica,* they informed the press that it was mere coincidence. When they turned up at some of the same night spots in Paris, they told the press that they traveled in the same circles. But when they stayed together, in the same hotel in Switzerland, the press finally ignored their denials and loudly heralded the new love affair throughout the world.

But before Rita Hayworth could marry Ali Khan, she had to pass the approval of the Aga Khan. The press waited breathlessly for the prospective father-in-law's ruling, and everyone was relieved when the American movie queen was declared A-OK with Aga.

The couple was married on May 27, 1949, at a family ceremony at

L'Horizon, Ali Khan's villa in Cannes. A civil ceremony was later performed at the city hall of Vallauris, France.

Ali Khan did not want to disappoint the press or Rita's fans. He announced that his honeymoon with Ms. Hayworth would be the most lavish, extensive, and expensive honeymoon of all time. The couple planned a lengthy tour of Europe, Africa, and Asia.

The honeymoon began in London. The couple then toured the countryside and went to Epsom Downs for the races. They departed from England for a motor tour of rural France.

The French tour was cut short by a new development—Rita was pregnant. Ali Khan bought a villa in Switzerland for the honeymooners to retreat to, and seven months later their daughter, Yasmin, was born.

Just weeks after his daughter's birth, Ali Khan announced that they would resume their honeymoon as planned, and the not-so-newlyweds flew off for an extensive tour of Africa.

But just about then, Columbia Pictures, who held Rita's contract, began to feel her absence. She had not made a new film in over a year. To soothe hurt feelings, Rita invited a film crew to document her honeymoon trip through Africa. The Hayworth-Khan honeymoon is the only real-life honeymoon to become a feature presentation at local theaters everywhere. Unfortunately, it is definitely rated PG.

Somewhere in the middle of Africa Rita got fed up with the honeymoon script and flew back to France. She established a single residence there and soon sued Ali Khan for divorce.

If one includes the expense of the Ali Khan divorce settlement, theirs becomes undeniably the world's most expensive honeymoon.

● ● ●

● Lana Turner's Eight Honeymoons ●

She was a Hollywood sex goddess and the original sweater girl. Discovered by a Hollywood talent agent while sitting at the counter of Schwab's Drug Store sipping a soda, she was signed up by MGM, who paraded her natural endowments in sweater after sweater, in a vast array of meaningless motion pictures.

Later in life, Lana Turner would make sensational headlines when her teenage daughter went to trial for the murder of Lana's gangland lover, Johnny Stampanato. The press and the public would remember her as the sweater girl, but forget the fact that she had already been married five times.

Husband number one was clarinet player Artie Shaw. Shaw married every Hollywood starlet he could get his hands on, who in the end totaled eight. (Later, Artie Shaw would marry and divorce Lana's rival film queen, Ava Gardner, and Gardner later married one of Lana's discarded husbands.)

Shaw and Lana had a whirlwind Hollywood courtship. He flew her to Las Vegas for a quick marriage in a rented private plane called "The Honeymoon Special." (Apparently, he had rented the plane before.) Lana wired her mother from Vegas to tell her she had been married, but she neglected to tell her to whom.

ALAN WEINBERG

The Shaw-Turner marriage made gossipy headlines as the number one Hollywood elopement of the year. Just as the press became bored with the story, Turner and Shaw were divorced. They had been married four months.

Several months after her first divorce, Lana met Stephen Crane, who was a major executive in a hot dog manufacturing company. Crane was wildly infatuated with Lana and asked her to marry him almost immediately. Lana agreed, and married Crane when she had known him only nine days.

They flew to Las Vegas. A large sign reading, Welcome Back, Lana, greeted them on their arrival. They were married by the same judge who had married Lana and Artie Shaw.

Unfortunately, in his haste and ardor, Crane forgot that his divorce from his first wife wasn't valid for another two months. Ms. Turner was unknowingly honeymooning with a genuine bigamist! To make matters worse, a month after her illegal marriage, Lana discovered that she was pregnant.

Crane and Lana divorced two months after their ill-advised marriage. Lana was furious about the bigamy and wanted nothing further to do with Crane. Crane begged her to remarry him once his divorce was final, but Lana was adamant in her refusals.

Saddened over his loss of Lana, Crane fell into a deep depression and attempted suicide by taking an overdose of sleeping pills. He was, fortunately, discovered by friends and rushed to the hospital. Lana was genuinely horrified by Crane's suicide attempt. She raced to his bedside and promised to remarry him.

Directly after Crane's recovery, he and Lana drove to Tijuana, Mexico, for her third wedding and honeymoon. Ironically, they were married under a sign that read, Legal Matters Adjusted.

A honeymoon, though, is somewhat more than a mere "legal matter." Lana and Crane were divorced again within the year.

Lana's fourth marriage was to millionaire sportsman Bob Topping. This time Lana tried to be a little more selective in her mate and more fastidious in her marriage plans. She was now at the height of her career.

The wedding was held at the Bel Air home of William Wilkerson, the agent who had discovered Lana. She wore a chantilly lace wedding gown and a lace embroidered cap, decorated with jewels. The newlyweds took an *almost* traditional honeymoon trip to London—Topping fouled things up a bit by trying to combine business with pleasure. He lost four hundred thousand dollars when he tried to introduce stock-car racing to the British Empire. Lana allowed herself to be used as an advertisement, posing in an orchid-colored outfit, by an orchid-colored sports car.

Mostly, Londoners were bored by the Toppings, but the English press loathed them and wrote scathing articles about the silly American millionaire and his movie queen. The Toppings got the message and cut their honeymoon short. This had been Lana's longest honeymoon to date, and the marriage lasted four-and-a-half years.

Film actor Lex Barker was Turner husband number five. At this point, Lana had become embarrassed by all her failed marriage attempts. She married Barker in a civil ceremony in Paris. She rushed to the wedding in a bright green dress, covering her face with a handkerchief. The press felt that Lana was giving mixed signals. They could understand that she might want her new marriage to go unnoticed, but why show up in bright green?

The Barkers began their "secret" honeymoon in Paris, where Lex Barker announced that he would give up playing Tarzan roles, for his bride. The newlyweds toured Europe, giving interviews to the press in every major city they visited. Several years later they had a "secret" divorce.

When Lana Turner married her sixth husband, Fred May, the general public had forgotten that she had already had five honeymoons. They watched as Lana endured the pain of her daughter's murder trial, and as the list of Lana's countless lovers came to light.

Fred May was an inconspicuous husband. He was a nice, quiet race horse owner, and the couple had a nice quiet wedding and a simple honeymoon in Carmel, California. But life with Fred May was *too* quiet for Lana, and after several years of marriage, the couple parted ways.

Soon another of Lana's marriages made headlines; it was now the seventh time. In 1965, at the age of forty-five, she married thirty-four-year-old Robert Eaton, who was "associated with motion picture production." Lana said of her seventh wedding, "Tears streamed down my cheeks." The wedding took place in Arlington, Virginia, at the home of Eaton's father, a retired Navy captain.

Lana wore a street-length peach-colored dress of Italian lace. She planted a tier of pale peach carnations in her still very blonde hair. The couple "honeymooned" in Palm Springs, although at this point in her marital excursions, Lana referred to it as a "vacation."

The vacation came to an abrupt halt when Lana suffered a severe attack of some kind in the middle of the night and was rushed to a local hospital. The original diagnosis was a heart attack brought on by the strain of trying to keep up with her athletic new husband. Later, when Lana's whole body broke out in a rash, the attack was re-diagnosed as an allergic reaction, though the doctors never determined what she was allergic to.

To make up for their thwarted vacation, the Eatons took a belated honeymoon in Acapulco. Lana had previously spent a lot of time in Acapulco with Johnny Stampanato and his gangster friends, and the trip conjured up many painful memories for her.

Once again, the Eatons cut short their honeymoon. This time they went to work on the TV series *The Survivors*, which Eaton produced and in which Lana starred. Eaton found himself gradually being pushed out of control of the series by Lana, and the couple soon separated. Eaton began working on a novel that less than loosely depicted Lana's life, career, and husbands. An angered Lana soon filed for divorce.

A month after her divorce from Eaton, Lana married Ronald Dante, a nightclub hypnotist whom she'd known for three weeks. Ronald was thirty-nine years old, but reported his age as forty-nine. Later, Dante claimed that he had dated and married Lana on a bet from a bartender. At the time they met, Lana was smoking heavily and Dante claimed that he could cure her smoking through hypnotism. He did for a while. But Lana and Dante divorced after a six-month honeymoon, and she went back to smoking.

Discussing her marriages candidly, Lana later said, "You know why I've been married so many times? Take the seven men. I could have lived with any of them, other than the father of my daughter, without that piece of paper. But I want it right on the table. I want it legal. I gotta marry 'em. Better I shouldn't maybe, but I did."

As for the future, Ms. Turner adds, "No more paperwork!"

• <u>The Many Honeymoons of Elizabeth Taylor</u> •

I never slept with a man I wasn't married to. How many women can make that claim?
—Elizabeth Taylor

Child star Elizabeth Taylor grew up very fast under the watchful eyes of her mother and Metro-Goldwyn-Mayer. At eighteen, the heroine of *Lassie Come Home* and *National Velvet* had developed an enormous bust and become sexually explosive. The Hollywood press exploited Liz's new, raging sexuality by teaming her up with every eligible bachelor in the movie community.

MGM wanted Liz to get married. So did her mother. Both parties wanted to be sure that virginal Liz did not get embroiled in a messy sex scandal. Everyone was relieved when Liz became engaged to hotel heir Conrad "Nicky" Hilton, Jr. Some Hollywood gossips had speculated that Liz married Hilton to get out from under the thumb of her domineering mother.

Conrad Hilton, Sr., was pleased with the match because his twenty-three-year-old son was a renowned playboy, continually generating publicity and embarrassing the Hilton family.

The senior Hilton hoped his son's marriage would help him to settle down, and MGM hoped the marriage would keep red-hot Liz cool. Hilton, Sr., happily babbled the engagement news to Louella Parsons, and the betrothal soon made the society pages of newspapers everywhere. When Liz was interviewed about her attraction to, and compatibility with, Nicky Hilton, she commented, "We both like ice cream."

They were married on May 6, 1950, in the Roman Catholic Church of the Good Shepherd on Santa Monica in Beverly Hills.

Liz's wedding gown was designed by her costumer at MGM, Helen Rose. The gown was a white satin negligee trimmed with rose point lace, with a matching cap. MGM assumed the cost of the wedding gown, the bridesmaid dresses, and Liz's entire trousseau. Hilton helped things along by giving the couple a wedding present of one hundred shares of Hilton Hotels stock.

The wedding was not without mishap. Bill Pawley, who had been previously engaged to Liz, showed up at her apartment right before the wedding and sent Liz into tears. Liz's mother threw him out, dried Liz's eyes, and helped her dress for the wedding. Then Liz tore her veil on the car door. It was adequately restitched.

Once safely inside the church, Liz and Nicky awaited the beginning of the wedding march as their cue to parade down the aisle. The march did not begin because the organ had broken down. The bride and groom continued to wait in the wings for a time, and then finally decided to march down the aisle, sans music.

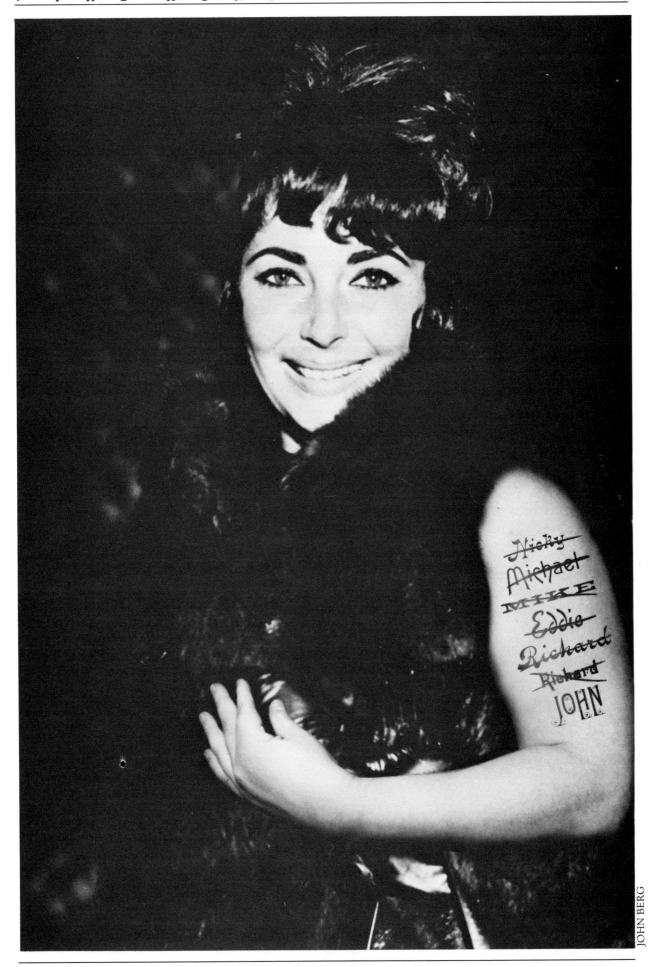

The Hilton honeymoon was highly publicized. After the wedding, the newlyweds had a brief stay at a golf club in Carmel, California. Then they were off to Paris for a much more glamorous honeymoon. When they left Carmel and flew to New York, reporters hounded them every minute.

A slight altercation occurred between the newlyweds when Nicky refused to pay the extra fee for Liz's excess baggage on their flight to New York. They were mobbed by reporters when they boarded the *Queen Mary* for their honeymoon cruise to Europe, and were disappointed to find out that the Duke and Duchess of Windsor had already booked the bridal suite.

Once in Paris, the bride and groom set up residence at the Hotel George V. International reporters again crowded around the honeymooners and asked Liz what she was carrying in her many trunks. "I don't know," she replied. "My mother packed them."

Nicky spent a great deal of time in France gambling, which was one of his passions. Unfortunately, Liz could not accompany him because she was underage (eighteen at the time) and not allowed inside the casinos.

It seemed apparent that the honeymoon was over as the newlyweds sailed back to New York on the *Queen Elizabeth*. Liz boarded the ship with seventeen trunks—apparently she had spent a lot of time alone in Paris buying clothes. Once aboard the ship, Nicky openly ignored Liz. He spent his time at the gaming tables, while she walked the decks alone. Occasionally, after dinner, she would ask total strangers to dance with her.

A year later they were divorced.

Liz met Michael Wilding in London where she was filming *Ivanhoe*. Wilding was a veteran actor of British films, who lived quietly and comfortably in London, but vowed that he was going to give up acting and move to the country to paint.

Liz admired his retiring ways, his acting ability, his intellectual appetite, and the fact that he was totally indifferent to her. She openly chased him around London for several months and then she proposed to him. Wilding was reluctant, at best. Most of his close friends could not figure out why he accepted her proposal. Wilding had no desire to move to California or become part of the Hollywood community.

Liz saw marriage to Wilding as an opportunity to settle down, have children, and lead a quiet life. Wilding was twenty years her senior, and Liz longed for a father figure.

They were married quietly at the Caxton Hall registry in London, in February 1952. Liz wore a sedate gray wedding outfit, again designed by Helen Rose and paid for by MGM. Wilding wondered how his British currency allowance of sixty dollars a month would ever pay for a suitable honeymoon for his glamorous new bride.

Liz wasn't interested in a honeymoon (her last one was quite enough, thank you), and she got pregnant right away. She had a baby boy before the end of the year. MGM realized that they hadn't lost their star, but had gained a talented British actor. The problem was what to do with him.

The Wildings moved to a small house near Hollywood, and Liz was still busy babymooning. Soon, a second son was born. Meanwhile, MGM cast Wilding in a series of horrible costume epics that did not do justice to his talent. He became quickly disillusioned with his life in California and bored with his marriage. He also developed an intense loathing of MGM.

The Wildings' marriage was really over before Mike Todd appeared on the scene. And once Wilding had to face competition for his movie-star wife, he gallantly stepped aside.

Ironically, Wilding did not go back to England to paint. He quit acting, and became an agent for actors (one of the "Hollywood types" he most loathed). Surprisingly, he spent the rest of his life in Hollywood.

When Liz announced her impending marriage to Mike Todd, Hedda Hopper quoted Todd as saying, "From now on, you'll know nobody but me." Only Hopper would openly admit that Todd didn't say "know."

He was known as "Todd, the Almighty," the magnificent producer and entrepreneur. Usually he got what he wanted through his charm and persuasiveness; sometimes through out-and-out thievery. Liz would later say that Mike Todd could "charm the gold out of your teeth."

Mike Todd never propsed to Liz. He simply told her that she was going to marry him. He announced their engagement to a star-studded audience at the premiere of *Around the World in Eighty Days*. Liz's engagement ring was a thirty-carat diamond worth ninety-two thousand dollars.

Todd flew his wedding party to Acapulco for the ceremony. The ceremony was Jewish, and Liz took some instruction in the new faith without actually converting. Helen Rose once again designed Liz's wedding dress, and MGM footed the bill. Todd and Liz were married on February 3, 1957.

Todd's close friend Eddie Fisher served as best man and sang "The Wedding Serenade." Mrs. Fisher, actress Debbie Reynolds, was Liz's matron of honor. At the time of the ceremony Liz had two slipped disks in her back and could barely walk. But she made it down the aisle like a seasoned pro.

On the Todds' wedding night, fireworks etched the newlyweds' initials in the darkened sky. "Todd, the Almighty" had lit up Acapulco for Liz.

Their honeymoon was as grandiose as one of Todd's own productions. They went around the world in eighty days to promote his film and their marriage. The press followed them everywhere. In mid-honeymoon, Liz announced her new pregnancy. Todd was barely able to contain his pleasure, and yelled to the press, "Stand back everyone. My wife is pregnant."

The press had a field day. They felt that Liz had finally met her match in Mike Todd. This was a honeymoon that would last forever.

A year and a half later, Mike Todd was killed in a plane crash.

It is often the case that a bereaved widow, following the death of her husband, will turn to the husband's best friend so that they may comfort and console each other. This was true of Eddie Fisher and Liz Taylor. But when the couple spent a clandestine week in the Catskills (at Grossinger's, no less) the press picked it up and blasted the news throughout the world. "Debbie and Eddie, Splitsville?" cried the tabloid headlines. "Taylor, a Marriage Wrecker!"

Debbie Reynolds denied all the rumors of her impending divorce, while Liz converted to Judaism. (This was probably more of a throwback to Mike Todd, than Eddie Fisher's influence.)

Liz married Fisher on May 12, 1959 in Las Vegas, where Fisher was performing. She said that she wanted to devote her time to being a wife and mother. This was the first Liz Taylor honeymoon that MGM had no part in financing. MGM did not relish the adverse publicity Liz had garnered, but it was undeniable that, as a "homewrecker," Liz had more clout at the box office than ever before.

Liz forced MGM to cast Fisher in her new movie *Butterfield 8*, and then to rewrite Fisher's part so it would have more importance. At the time, Liz was being offered a million dollars from Twentieth Century-Fox to play Cleopatra, so MGM abided by her wishes.

Liz divided her honeymoon with Eddie Fisher between work and the hospital. After the publicity began to die down, she and Fisher hurriedly filmed *Butterfield 8*. Soon she was off to Europe to begin filming *Cleopatra*. The woman who wanted to devote her time to being a wife and mother collapsed with pneumonia in the middle of the European filming. Her doctors blamed the attack on exhaustion brought on by too much honeymooning, publicity, and work.

Directly following the pneumonia attack Liz would begin a new honeymoon, this time with Richard Burton. Once again, Liz made worldwide headlines. Eddie bowed out calmly, stating, "I won't stand in the lady's way." Burton wasn't so quick to give up his own marriage, and the world got to watch Liz chase him around for several amusing years before Burton gave Liz her fifth honeymoon. As a result of all the publicity he received, Burton became a widely sought after, highly paid actor. He could well afford to marry Liz, and did so in Montreal in 1964. To solve Liz's great religious confusion, the wedding ceremony in Montreal was Unitarian. Soon Burton began buying every large diamond he could get his hands on for his bride, and Liz became the most lavishly bejeweled honeymooner in the world.

This time, Liz had married a true film partner, and they spent a great deal of their honeymoon flying around the world co-starring with each other. At first they played romantic couples with problems. Year by year, one could watch the Burton marriage enacted on film. Each year the film romances and marriages became more and more destructive. After seven years, the films began to flop at the box office, and so did their marriage. They were divorced in 1974.

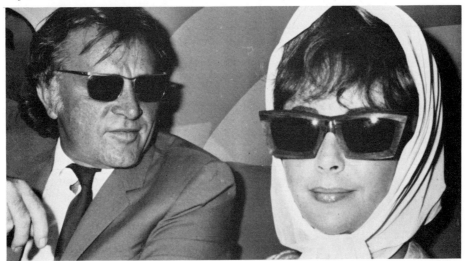

Like true showmen, the Burtons attempted a comeback. The very next year they surprised us all by remarrying.

The comeback was well staged. They had flown to Israel, to party with Henry Kissinger. The couple then journeyed to South Africa to attend a black tennis tournament, the press following along as part of their entourage. Liz had never liked to travel and sleep with a man she wasn't married to and insisted that Burton remarry her immediately. Burton really didn't have any intention of remarrying Liz, and stayed drunk through most of the African tour.

But once when he was in a sober moment Liz nailed him, and they remarried in Botswana, in a wedding service they had written themselves. Liz was decked out in a Druid wedding dress trimmed with beads and feathers, and Burton added another large diamond to Liz's ever growing collection. This honeymoon Liz ended up spending in divorce court, when three weeks later the couple decided to separate.

In 1976, Liz married John Warner, a Republican congressman from Virginia. They settled into married life together at his home in the Blue Ridge Mountains. Liz enjoyed the honeymoon of a political wife, and spent her time shaking hands, kissing babies, and shopping in the supermarket. In a show of married solidarity, Liz and Warner even picked out grave sites together. Though formerly a Democrat (and a liberal one at that), Liz has totally immersed herself in her new starring role. With her movie career all but finished, this seems to be a very good part for her, but who really knows?

♥   ♥   ♥

● The Honeymoon of Marilyn Monroe and Joe DiMaggio ●

Marilyn Monroe married Joe DiMaggio on January 14, 1954, in the San Francisco city hall. It was a match made in heaven. America's favorite macho baseball hero ties the knot with America's favorite sex kitten.

DiMaggio wore a dark suit with the same polka dot tie he had worn the night he met Marilyn. He referred to it as his "lucky tie." Marilyn was sedately dressed in a brown suit with a tall ermine collar. DiMaggio had warned Marilyn to "save the low-cut things for the movies."

The newlyweds spent their wedding night at a motel on Highway 101 outside Paso Robles. Then they pressed on to a friend's mountain lodge near Palm Springs, where they spent a few blissful, publicity-free days.

Because of her refusal to play a part in what she considered an insipid movie called *Pink Tights*, Marilyn was spending her honeymoon on suspension from Twentieth Century-Fox. The bride and groom soon left the mountain lodge to return to the DiMaggio family's two-story house in the Marina district of San Francisco.

Marilyn was spared the horrors of immediate domesticity. DiMaggio's sister did all the cooking and housework. Marilyn used this stay in San Francisco as a rest period before her formal honeymoon trip to Japan.

DiMaggio was to make a public relations tour of Japanese baseball teams, and Twentieth Century-Fox decided that they would forgive Marilyn if she made some nice wholesome honeymoon headlines with her hero husband.

The newlyweds flew first to Honolulu, where Marilyn was mobbed by

Marriaggio

年逢を熟纱王

由名裥

甲名裥敬

GENE GREIF

fans and DiMaggio attracted little interest. This would be his first experience of being upstaged by Marilyn. Then they were off to Tokyo to attend to DiMaggio's business.

On the evening of their arrival in Tokyo, Marilyn and DiMaggio attended a cocktail party held in their honor. Several U.S. Army officers approached Marilyn, asking her if she would take a few days to fly to Korea to entertain the American combat troops. How could Marilyn refuse? It would have been un-American! The next day she left a brooding DiMaggio, and flew off to Seoul.

From Seoul, she was taken by helicopter into the war zone. It was freezing, but Marilyn made her entrance dangling from the helicopter in what could be called, only by a stretch of the imagination, a low-cut dress. She was dropped onto the stage to the roar and applause of loving servicemen. Scantily clad and shivering in the twenty-degree weather, she warbled "Diamonds Are a Girl's Best Friend." She sang it very badly, but none of the GI's cared.

Marilyn was so thrilled with the adulation she had received from the GI's that she agreed to tour the Korean battle zone for a few more shows. She called DiMaggio and asked him to join her, but he had already been infuriated by her departure and stubbornly refused to come. Marilyn stayed on in Korea without him.

When she finally returned to Tokyo, Marilyn was running a fever of a hundred and four and soon developed a mild case of pneumonia. Those chilly performances, and the exhaustion of the impromptu tour, left her weakened and ill for the rest of her stay in Japan.

Thousands of American GI's had been enthralled. Twentieth Century-Fox had gotten its all-American publicity. But, Joe DiMaggio was less than thrilled with his honeymoon.

● Two-Time Honeymoons- ● Couples Who Honeymooned Together Twice

● William Saroyan and Carol Marcus ●

Saroyan once explained his twice-failed marriage this way: "In 1942, I met her at last, in 1943 I married her, in 1949 I divorced her. In 1951, I married her again, I divorced her in 1952, and then I didn't marry her anymore." But Walter Matthau did, in 1959.

● Milton Berle and Joyce Mathews ●

The first marriage lasted six years, the second, nine months. Berle later commented, "It was as if we had gone straight from the altar to the rocks." Joyce Mathews then repeated her marital performance with Billy Rose.

● Billy Rose and Joyce Mathews ●

Showman Billy Rose had divorced his swimming-star wife, Eleanor Holm, to marry Joyce Mathews. The press called it "the new War of the Roses." They were divorced thirty-seven months after their wedding, and remarried two years later. Billy Rose commented, "She was living in my house, anyway."

● Dorothy Parker and Alan Campbell ●

It was remarked at the Parker-Campbell remarriage that most of the guests hadn't spoken to each other in years! The first marriage had lasted four-teen years. The two were divorced for three years, and then honeymooned until Alan Campbell's death. Everyone is entitled to a little time off for bad behavior.

● Natalie Wood and Robert Wagner ●

Young boy star meets young girl star. They marry and honeymoon for five years. Boy star loses girl star, they each marry someone else, and have babies. Suddenly they mature, become disillusioned with their present partner, and get divorced. Boy star gets girl star again. They marry again and live happily ever after.

♥ What Some Celebrities Had to Say About Their Own Honeymoon ♥

♥ Hubert Humphrey ♥

"We took sixty-five dollars and my father's car for a honeymoon trip to Minneapolis and northern Minnesota. On the way back to South Dakota, we hit and killed a cow. So we came home dragging behind a tow truck, and a debt to a dairy farmer. But I'd do it the same way all over again."

♥ Woody Allen ♥

"I'd like to honeymoon in Mexico. I loved it last year when I was there for my divorce."

♥ Maggie Smith ♥

"I absolutely refuse to discuss it or elaborate on it, but it just so happens that I fell into a swimming pool."

♥ David Niven ♥

"Honeymoons are like dreams. You wake up and find it either impossible or quite ridiculous to remember them."

♥ Jack Warden ♥

"I got the hiccups and couldn't stop until I went for a walk and was frightened by a German shepherd."

♥ Bette Davis ♥

"In my day, a woman never said a word about what happened on her honeymoon, or honeymoons, as the case may be."

♥ Mia Farrow ♥

"During one honeymoon the bridegroom kept asking me if I was all right. I kept saying yes. Then at a particular moment, he asked again if I was all right and I said no, for a change. He was mystified the rest of the honeymoon."

♥ Frankie Avalon ♥

"It was a heavenly delight! And since I was a teen angel I should know."

♥ Paul McCartney ♥

"The tourists wouldn't leave us alone. We got homesick."

♥ Tony Perkins ♥

"My wife's dog bit me when he jumped on the bed. As for where—never mind!"

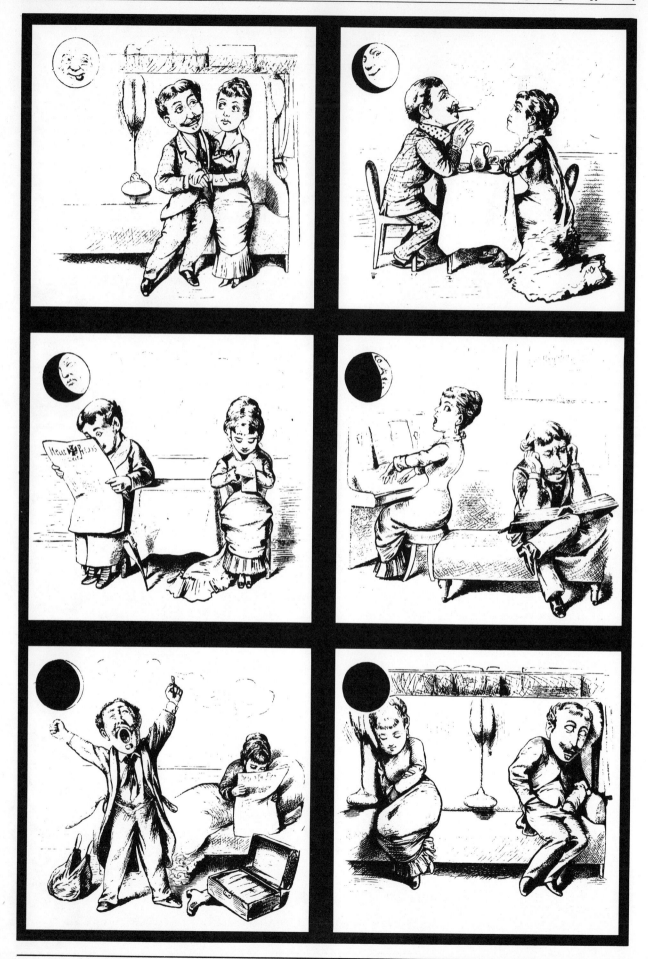

CHAPTER EIGHT

THE HONEYMOON IS OVER

Another year,
Or maybe less,
What's this I hear,
well can't you guess?
She feels neglected
And he's suspected
of makin' whoopee.

He doesn't make much money
Only five thousand per
Some judge who thinks he's funny
Says he'll have to pay six to her.

The boy says "Judge,
Suppose I fail?"
The Judge says "Son,
Right into jail.
You better keep her,
I think it's cheaper,
Than makin' whoopee."

Honeymoons, like all good things, must come to an end. Though we all fervently strive to honeymoon through life, at some point the routine of day-to-day living interferes with our constant quest for romance. Suddenly, and subtly, the honeymoon is over, and we have settled down to secure and sometimes boring married life.

Here are some warning signals of impending disaster.

♥ The honeymoon is over when he phones that he'll be late again for dinner, and she has already left a note that his dinner is in the refrigerator.

♥ The honeymoon is over when the wife starts complaining about the noise he makes preparing his breakfast.

♥ The honeymoon is over when she starts wondering what happened to the man she married, and he starts wondering what happened to the girl he didn't.

♥ The honeymoon is over when he stops helping her with the dishes and starts doing them himself.

♥ The honeymoon is over when the man discovers his wife isn't an angel, so he quits posing as a saint.

♥ The honeymoon is over when he takes her off a pedestal and puts her on a budget.

♥ The honeymoon is over the first time he says, "You'll do nothing of the kind!"

♥ The honeymoon is over when she stops lowering her eyes and starts raising her voice.

♥ The honeymoon is over when the couple who took each other for better or for worse start taking each other for granted.

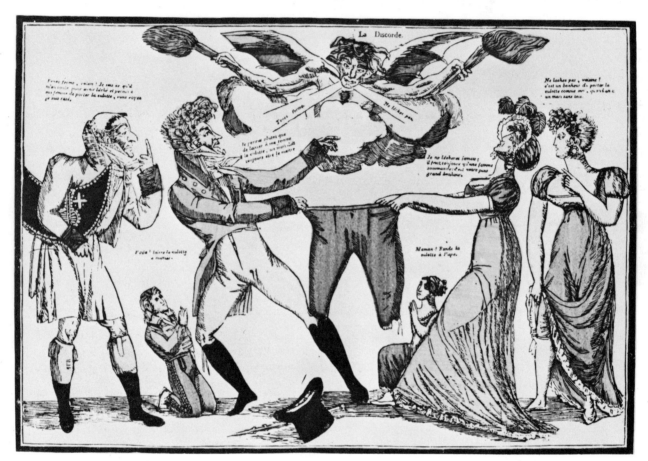

And now that marriage has become a reality, the following words of wisdom are a good indication of what all the honeymooners have gotten themselves into.

♥ The bonds of matrimony are like any other bonds: they mature slowly.

♥ No matter how happily a woman may be married, it always pleases her that there is some nice man who wishes she weren't.

♥ It takes two to make marriage a success, and only one to make it a failure.

♥ Some newlyweds quarrel on their honeymoon, but most couples don't settle down to married life so quickly.

♥ The great secret of a successful marriage is to treat all disasters as incidents, and none of the incidents as disasters.

Lily Tomlin

If love is the answer, could you rephrase the question?

When two people marry they become in the eyes of the law one person, and that person is the husband.
—Shana Alexander

Love means never having to say you're sorry.
—Erich Segal

I haven't known any open marriages, though quite a few have been ajar.

Bob Hope

Take my wife. Please.
—Henny Youngman

Open marriage is nature's way of telling you that you need a divorce.
—Marshall Brickman

A woman without a man is like a fish without a bicycle.

You never really know a man until you've divorced him.

I sleep well when Bella is in Washington. I sleep even better when she is in Cambodia.
—Martin Abzug

Gloria Steinem

Marriage is the alliance of two people, one of whom never remembers birthdays, and the other never forgets them.
—Ogden Nash

Zsa Zsa Gabor

Marriage isn't an up- or -down issue. It's a side-by -side one.
—Prince Charles

I am a marvelous housekeeper. Every time I leave a man, I keep his house.

It takes two to destroy a marriage.
—Margaret Trudeau

Sometimes I wonder if men and women really suit each other. Perhaps they should live next door and just visit now and then.

Marrying a man is like buying something you've been admiring in a shop window. You may love it when you bring it home, but it doesn't always go with everything else in the house.
—Jean Kerr

Katharine Hepburn

Some married couples say, why don't we try twin beds instead of a double bed? We just went a little further and said, "Let's live in separate houses."
—William Proxmire

Love is so much better when you are not married.

It all comes down to who does the dishes.

Norman Mailer

We sleep in separate bedrooms, we have dinner apart, we take separate vacations. We're doing everything we can to keep our marriage together.
—Rodney Dangerfield

Maria Callas

The best of all possible marriages is a seesaw in which first one then the other partner is dominant.
—Dr. Joyce Brothers

It is true that I never should have married, but I didn't want to live without a man. Brought up to respect the conventions, love had to end in marriage. I'm afraid it did.
—Bette Davis

♥ Marriage is like paying an endless visit in your worst clothes.

♥ A happy marriage is a long conversation that seems all too short.

♥ Getting married, like getting hanged, is a great deal less dreadful than it is made out to be.

♥ Marriage is the most licentious of human institutions, and that is the secret of its popularity.

♥ The trouble with wedlock is that there is not enough wed, and too much lock.

♥ It is no disgrace for a woman to make a mistake in marrying; every woman does it.

♥ He who marries best puts it off until it is too late.

♥ Every girl waits for the right man to come along, but in the meantime she gets married.

♥ Marriage is singular: you add one and one, and you get one.

♥ Married life is a mistake: first he talks, then she talks, and then the neighbors talk.

♥ The only thing worse than marrying a man to reform him is marrying a woman to educate her.

♥ Marriage is an unfailing method of turning an ardent admirer into a carping critic.

♥ The trouble with matrimony is not with the institution. It's with the personnel.

♥ Married life is like sitting in a bathtub. Once you get used to it, it's not so hot.

♥ Whoever said that marriage is a fifty-fifty proposition doesn't know the half of it.

♥ Matrimony is the most effective reducing diet yet discovered for a swelled head.

♥ Marriage is like a cafeteria. You pick out something that looks good and pay later.

♥ Marriage is an investment that always pays dividends, but only if you pay interest.

MARRIAGE IS—

♥ A friendship recognized by the police. —Robert Louis Stevenson

♥ A world-without-end bargain. —William Shakespeare

♥ The most expensive way to get your laundry done. —Charles James

♥ Alas! Another instance of the triumph of hope over experience. —Dr. Samuel Johnson

I never loved another person the way I love myself.

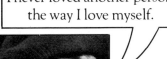
Mae West

No one ever filed for divorce on a full stomach. —Mamma Leone

There is one thing more exasperating than a wife who can cook, and won't, and that's the wife who can't cook, and will. —Robert Frost

When I can no longer think of the victims of broken homes, I begin to think of the victims of intact ones. —Peter DeVries

Pat Boone

We all suffer from the preoccupation that there exists in the loved one perfection.

When you get married, you forget about kissing other women.

To catch a husband is an art; to hold him is a job. —Simone de Beauvoir

Throughout history, women have picked providers for mates. Men pick anything.

In an age when the fashion is to be in love with yourself, confessing to being in love with somebody else is an admission of unfaithfulness to one's beloved. —Russell Baker

Sidney Poitier

The happiest time of anyone's life is just after the first divorce. John Kenneth Galbraith

Marriage is a half step—a way of leaving home without losing home. —Gail Sheehy

Men often marry their mothers. —Edna Ferber

A man's home may seem to be his castle on the outside; inside it's more often his nursery.

Margaret Mead

Behind every successful man you'll find a woman who has nothing to wear.

We haven't ruled the possibility of children out. I figure I'm the blessed event in our family. —Dick Cavett

A wife, so often, is her mother. —Gail Sheehy

As usual, there's a great woman behind every idiot. —John Lennon

Jimmy Stewart

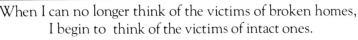
Clare Boothe Luce

For some reason, it seems that the bride generally has to make more of an effort to achieve a successful marriage than the bridegroom. —Elizabeth Post

The art of love is largely the art of persistence. —Dr. Albert Einstein

A man in love is not complete until he's married. Then he's finished.

My wife's jealousy is getting ridiculous. The other day she looked at my calendar and demanded to know who May was. —Rodney Dangerfield

God is a maker of marriages, but I wonder if He would bother to come to some of the affairs He has arranged? —Harry Golden

Love in marriage is a commitment. Commitment involves a woman's full surrender to her man. —Marabel Morgan

Time in love and time in life are unrelated; forever exists more than once. —Ned Rorem

Why does a woman work ten years to change a man's habits, and then complain that he's not the man she married? —Barbra Streisand

I will never make a statement that I wouldn't remarry. —Elizabeth Taylor

Zsa Zsa Gabor

THE KIND OF A GIRL
A MAN MARRIES

THE KIND OF A WIFE
HE EXPECTS HER TO BE

> ♥ *Our fond lovers are now united; and as the honeymoon is over, it becomes necessary for them to come down from their romance, and enter upon the sober duties of a married life.*
>
> It was not long, therefore, before her husband began to experience little annoyances, in consequence of her want of domestic knowledge. The wife still imagines that all the power and peculiar influence which she possessed over him in the sweetheart-state must of right continue. From this false view, induced by the self-sacrificing devotion of the lover, much unhappiness flows when the sweetheart becomes the wife.
>
> The sweeping and dusting were carelessly done, and the furniture, from want of attention, began to look a little dingy, much to the annoyance of Mrs. Fairfield. Still, it did not occur to her that she was wrong in leaving everything to her servants.
>
> Too frequently he was kept from his store in the morning, half an hour later than his business required him to be there, in consequence of breakfast not being ready. Whenever this happened, he usually hurried away without the parting kiss.
>
> "I fear he does not love me!" the young wife would often say, bursting into tears, as she closed her chamber door after her, and sat down to weep in abandonment of feelings.
>
> —T. S. Arthur, "Sweethearts and Wives," in *Godey's Lady's Book* (1841)

♥ Many a man lives by the sweat of his frau.　　　—Anonymous

♥ *It is always incomprehensible to a man that a woman should ever refuse an offer of marriage.*　　　—Jane Austen

♥ Marriage has teeth, and him bite very hot.　　　—Jamaican Proverb

♥ A rich bride goes young to the church.　　　—Old German Proverb

> ♥ *I believe that the marriage institution, like slavery and monarchy, and many other things which have been good or necessary in their day, is now effete, and in a general sense injurious, instead of being beneficial, to the community, although of course it must continue to linger until better institutions can be formed. I mean by marriage in this connection, any forced or obligatory tie.*　　—*Victoria Woodhull (1872)*

♥ Wedlock: The deep, deep peace of the double bed after the hurly-burly of the chaise lounge.　　　—Mrs. Patrick Campbell

♥ One college president boasted that before hiring a new faculty or administrative staff member, he insisted on having breakfast with the candidate's family. It was his judgment that if the wife "didn't fix her husband a good breakfast," the man "wasn't a good risk."
　　　—Robert Seidenberg, M.D., *Corporate Wives—Corporate Casualties*

♥ An executive's wife should watch her figure and don't nag.
　　　—A Ford Motor Company Executive

♥ Ilo Wallace told me that on the day of their marriage, Henry's father, who had been secretary of agriculture under both Harding and Coolidge, had given them a wedding present of a new Ford. She and Henry came out of the church after the ceremony, and Henry was so pleased with the sight of the Ford that he ignored the kissers and congratulators, went immediately to the car, and drove off. It was thought odd, but people said he was testing it for her comfort until a half hour passed, and then another. Toward the late afternoon he returned, and called out from the driver's seat, "Get in, Ilo, I'd forgotten you."

—Lillian Hellman, *Scoundrel Time*

♥ So you are with the army now!...Although no serviceman's career was ever made by his wife, many have been hindered or helped by the social skills of their wives, their flexibility, and their loyalty toward the army and its customs....As an army wife, never forget that you are the "silent" member of the team, but a key "man." You belong to a strong team that has never lost a war (if you think we lost Vietnam, ask some West Pointers), so take pride in the aims and ideals of the U.S. Army....Marriage is the most important legal agreement you will ever make. —*The Army Wife*, a book given by the U.S. Army to brides before their military wedding.

Let there be spaces in your togetherness. —*Kahlil Gibran*, The Prophet

A "Life" cartoon lampooned the figures in arranged matches: the heiress bound by her mother's will, the smallish nobleman, the preacher blind to the travesty.

♥ The women of America, who often exhibit a masculine strength of understanding and manly energy, generally preserve great delicacy of personal appearance and always retain the manners of women....I do not hesitate to avow that, if I were asked, to what singular prosperity and growing strength of this people ought mainly to be attributed, I should reply—to the superiority of their women.

—Alexis de Tocqueville, *On American Women and American Wives* (1830)

♥ When I first met my wife, she was a schoolteacher. I used to write her passionate love letters—and she'd send them back corrected. I must be the only man in the world who returned from his honeymoon and received a report card. It said: Dick is neat and friendly and shows a keen interest in fun and games.   —Dick Lord, Comedian

Some pray to marry the man they love,
My prayer will somewhat vary:
I humbly pray to Heaven above
That I love the man I marry.
—Rose Pastor Stokes, "My Prayer"

♥ Since it is inevitable that most of us will at one time or another commit the folly of marriage, we might as well have a sense of humor about it. These jokes and stories are as timeless as the institution they mock.

RUTH: I, too, had an ideal once.
ROSE: How did you come to lose it?
RUTH: I married it.

GOVERNMENT OFFICER: Are you married or single?
APPLICANT: Married
OFFICER: Where were you married?
APPLICANT: I don't know.
OFFICER: You don't know where you were married?
APPLICANT: Oh, I thought you said, *why.*

MRS. JONES: Does your husband remember your wedding anniversary?
MRS. SMITH: No. So I remind him of it in January and June, and get two presents.

♥ With a charming air of romance and pleasant sentimentality, the company were discussing how each of the married couples among them had first met.

"And where did you first meet your wife?" the little man in the corner was asked.

"Gentlemen, I did not meet her," he replied solemnly. "She overtook me."

♥ "Jack's getting terribly absentminded. Just the other day he kissed a woman by mistake."

"Thought it was his wife, eh?"

"No, it was his wife."

♥ "A husband leads a dog's life," said Mr. Allen.

"That's right," agreed Mrs. Allen. "He growls all day, and snores all night."

♥ On the occasion of her silver wedding anniversary, a woman was congratulated by a minister for living so many years with the same man.

"But he's not the same man he was when I got hold of him." she replied.

♥ "Henry," whispered his wife, "I'm convinced there's a burglar downstairs.

"Well, my dear," replied the husband drowsily, "I hope you don't expect me to have the courage of your convictions."

♥ The young bride was asked what she thought about married life.

"Oh, there's not much difference," she replied. "I used to wait up half the night for George to go home, and now I wait up half the night for him to come home."

For further edification, here are the ten most serious grievances husbands and wives have about one another, in the order of the most massive irritation:

HUSBANDS' COMPLAINTS ABOUT WIVES	WIVES' COMPLAINTS ABOUT HUSBANDS
1. Nags me	1. Is selfish and inconsiderate
2. Isn't affectionate	2. Is unsuccessful in business
3. Is selfish and inconsiderate	3. Is untruthful
4. Complains too much	4. Complains too much
5. Interferes with my hobbies	5. Doesn't show his affection
6. Is slovenly in appearance	6. Doesn't talk things over
7. Is quick tempered	7. Is harsh with the children
8. Interferes with my discipline	8. Is very touchy
9. Is conceited	9. Has no interest in children
10. Is insincere	10. Has no interest in the home

SENSUAL PLEASURE HAS THE FLEETING BRILLIANCE OF A
COMET; A HAPPY MARRIAGE HAS THE TRANQUILLITY OF
A LOVELY SUNSET.

Paula Scher was born in Washington D.C. and raised in suburban Maryland. She graduated from Tyler School of Art (Temple University) where she majored in graphic design.

Ms. Scher is currently Senior Art Director for CBS Records. Her record covers, posters, and advertising design have garnered her virtually every existing graphic design award including four Grammy nominations for cover of the year.

The Honeymoon Book is Scher's second book, her first being a children's book called "The Brownstone."